THE FIVE A'S
OF GREAT EMPLOYEES

*Breakthrough Strategies for
Hiring and Managing People*

ERIC SWENSON

The Five A's of Great Employees: Breakthrough Strategies for Hiring and Managing People

Published by Wheatmark®
1760 East River Road, Suite 145
Tucson, Arizona 85718 USA
www.wheatmark.com

ISBN: 978-1-62787-265-2 (paperback)
ISBN: 978-1-62787-266-9 (ebook)
LCCN: 2015956224

CONTENTS

CONTENTS

PART 3
Using the Five A's to Manage Employees
103

Appendix
115

Acknowledgments

I've spent most of the last thirty years of my professional career studying and trying to understand how people can work at their best—to their potential, with each other, and to maximize productivity and happiness for both the individual and the business for whom they work. I didn't do this by going to classes; I did it in the real world.

Working with a variety of CEOs, executives, managers, and business owners has been an education in and of itself. The great ones are always learning and never satisfied with the status quo. The smartest CEO I have ever worked with ends every meeting or call by asking, "What can I do better?"

Trying to hire and retain the best possible people is a combination of many attributes: a great talent acquisition and selection process; superior managers who understand that success is predicated on the success of the people who work for and with them; and being honest enough to decide quickly who should stay and who should go.

One of the great joys in consulting to businesses is being able to see so many different approaches to talent management, then taking the best approaches and refining them and relating them to other businesses. It's not really rocket science: It is recognizing what works and what does not and having the courage to try (and fail) frequently.

While interviewing alone is not the only way to identify talent, it is the most common, and therefore what I reference frequently in this book.

I have interviewed a lot of people in my career — and I do mean "a lot." My best guess is that I have interviewed or screened over five thousand applicants. I've studied the art, evaluated processes, assessed tests, and read books — one of which dedicates six hundred pages to the art of interviewing. My knowledge — and therefore my thanks — begins with the innovators, entrepreneurs, and authors who developed these systems and documented their research.

Today, most of the interviewing I do is on behalf of my clients, who also allow me to evaluate their existing employees. To these clients, I am forever grateful for the opportunity to practice my life's passion.

I am also fortunate to spend time with interviewees, who confide in me their own passions so that I can link their needs and wants with those businesses which pay me to improve their talent and leadership.

The stories in this book are true. Though some of the distinguishing characteristics have been changed, the clients, colleagues, and friends about whom these stories are based will recognize themselves. You know who you are, and I am forever indebted to you!

Phase One of my professional life was spent working for two large corporations. Phase Two has — thus far — been spent working with hundreds of businesses, from a start-up tech firm in a garage with more dogs than employees to businesses with thousands of employees. I'm often asked with what types of companies I prefer to work. Without exception, the answer is this: I prefer working with companies when the CEO, owner, or principal *gets it*. This means: when the top person in the company understands that doing the right thing is the right thing to do, and that doing what you ought to do will save you a lot of have-to-do's in your life. A sincere thank you to all of those companies who truly get it.

Thanks to my business partners, who stuck with me through some really brutal times. I'd especially like to single out Jake Jacobs: He and I have spent the last seven years alternating our thoughts between murder and love. I'm glad neither has happened.

Also thanks to Shana Merrill: I never really believed in reverse mentoring until I got to know Shana. For every piece of advice I've given her, it's been returned ten-fold. I'm exceptionally grateful.

I wouldn't have written this book, or be where I am today, without Tony Rose. Tony has vision, understanding, and, most of all, loyalty. And loyalty ranks very high on my friendship scale.

I love my team at RSJ/Swenson as well, with special thanks to Jamie Baker.

I wrote my first book, *Managing People in the 21st Century*, in 2003 at the age of 40, right after I quit my corporate management job and started my own business without a single client. I was clearly out of my mind. I thanked then, and thank now, my parents for their unconditional love and support.

One day soon, I hope to complete projects with two significant influencers in my business life: Michael Josephson has been a guidepost in my professional life for many years, first on the radio, and subsequently in our personal and professional meetings and discussions. Every moment I spend with him is impactful, and he is responsible for my beliefs towards insisting on honesty and ethics when it comes to aligning employees and employers

Jennifer Kushell is one of the smartest people I know. She has devoted her career to youth, millennials, and entrepreneurs — the people who will be (and, in many cases are) the future constituents of this book. In fact, it's fair to say that millennials, and what I have learned about them through my work with Jennifer, have driven each of The Five A's.

I have yet to meet Mel Kleiman, but I read his blogs and articles constantly, and he has been a big influencer on some of my hiring theories.

Jocelyn Baker has been part sounding board, part critic, and part editor throughout the preparation of the book. I couldn't have done it without her.

And finally, to Yukiji Kushida Swenson, an amazing person and incredible partner in life: Thanks for keeping me on my toes and focusing me on what is important.

Eric Swenson
Los Angeles, California
January 2016

PART 1

THE IMMUTABLE
MARK OF CHANGE

Until very recently, jobs were created for life. People stayed at a job because they had the ability to do that job. With years of experience under their belts, they were hard to replace. My great uncle, for instance, was a clerk at a department store for thirty years. His knowledge of that corporate culture made him nearly irreplaceable. Stock brokers, bankers, salesmen: These were jobs for life.

With such drastically low turnover, not often did the need arise for an employer to hire a new employee. When hiring became necessary, the employer looked for one thing: experience. Was this person able to do this job?

A lot of employees still feel that way—they go into a job thinking it will never change. A lot of employers view this similarly: They look for the best possible employee with the most experience for the job they have available today.

Neither is correct. Employers can no longer afford to hire for today. They need to hire for what it will look like next year, or five years from now. That's the person to look for.

Here's the brutal truth, whether you are an employee

or employer: Experience no longer counts. It's about what you are capable of doing tomorrow that's far more critical.

Today, no employer cares whether you have ten years of experience—especially when the technology, processes, and modus operandi they use are only two years old. Thanks to massive leaps in technology, every industry gets a makeover every few years, and this will continue until the end of time. Although a number of business owners and employees are slow to realize this fact, there isn't an exception to this rule. Take the banking industry: Banks are not exactly known for changing quickly or being on the forefront of new techniques. But even banks are starting to understand that they need employees who are willing to learn new things and who can adapt to the inescapable changes and chaos within the industry.

So this evolution is not limited to one industry, nor is it a passing fad. This seismic change has occurred globally and structurally. Technology has left an immutable mark on the face of employment culture: We will never revert to the old way of doing things. Consider the impact of technology on your employee turnover. Thanks to the Internet, your employees know how much they can make at a competing firm down the street. They know what former employees think of you and your company, and they know what former employees think of your competitors. At their fingertips, they have thousands of want-ads from all across the country.

All this information makes it easy for your employees to leave your firm. Gone forever are the days when a person could start a job fresh out of college and expect to stay with that company until given a gold watch at age sixty-five. Employees no longer have that loyalty.

Part of the reason they no longer have that loyalty is because businesses no longer have that loyalty. Given the fluctuation of the market in both the public and private sectors, employees' salaries are the first of the expenses to be eliminated at the hint of a bad fiscal quarter. Mergers, acquisitions, takeovers, consolidations and "re-organizations" threaten jobs every day. Most businesses today will no longer exist in thirty years—or, at least, they will look fundamentally different from what they do today, employing people with entirely different skill sets.

Hiring, then, is critical. Not only do you want to hand-select employees who are likely to stay on board for more than a little while, but you also want employees who will blow you out of the water in terms of performance. You need to find employees who have the characteristics that your firm needs, and you must also find those who have the potential to perform in the face of change.

Simply put, you are going to be hiring a lot more often, and a lot more differently, than your counterpart from just a decade ago.

Unfortunately, most businesses still look at employees and job candidates through the same lens as they did two or three decades ago. They review résumés and interview using the same old questions. They look for experience and technical competency as if these are the only criteria needed in this world of massive and constant change.

Today, we are confronted with a multi-cultural and multi-generational workforce with investors and shareholders demanding more profits, lower expenses, and better efficiency. In an era of social media, every employee and every customer are now broadcasters, having the ability and ease to shout their complaints or problems to millions of people.

Today's employees are significantly different from those who came before, and employers have significantly different needs from what they ever had before.

Employees demand more from their employers than ever before—because they can.

Customers expect more than ever before—because they can.

And we expect more of ourselves—because we should.

This is the new reality. We can no longer afford to tolerate employees who are less than excellent. Hiring better employees, reducing turnover, and insisting on excellence should be top business priorities.

But if ability and experience are no longer the Holy Grail in hiring, what is? Given that our needs today will be substantially different from what they are in five years, what marks the difference between a great employee and a mediocre employee?

I call them the Five A's.

THE ACTUAL MOST IMPORTANT THING

Every unacceptable employee was once someone you were excited to hire.

All of those well-intended people who have families to support but are nonetheless falling short, and whom you have nervously called into your office to terminate over the years, were once important enough to be offered jobs at your firm. All of the human disasters — the people who caused rifts, the ones who threatened your corporate culture, and the disgruntled ex-employees who filed lawsuits — were people you once believed would elevate your firm.

Today, right now, you have people working in your firm who are showing the early warning signs of being unacceptable employees. If you are like most employers, you might be brushing these telltale signs under the rug or rationalizing them — for now. You might even be paying employees whom you *know* you need to terminate, if only you could find the courage.

Never has a time existed when CEOs or business owners haven't lamented that some of their employees do not have what it takes. They complain about their employees' poor work ethic, lack of ability, and bad attitude. They want employees who are passionate, driven, and efficient. They long for the days when employees held themselves "accountable."

But if the employer—who should know his or her corporate culture, values, and firm's needs better than anyone—is also the person ultimately in charge of hiring and leading, then who is really to blame for having employees who are ill-suited for the job?

Certainly, the blame cannot lay entirely with the employees, most of whom have set out to find the most rewarding jobs available. They certainly do not hope for their days to be unfulfilling. They do not dream of sitting around idly and going through the motions at meaningless jobs for the sole purpose of collecting paychecks.

But, more often than not, employers—the only people who have the context to decide whether a candidate is a good fit—fail to have a system for identifying the right employees.

Here is a scenario that might sound familiar: A key employee has just given notice. Management sees a critical and urgent need to replace the employee, saying, "We need a body in there right now."

And thus begins a cycle of mediocrity: The rush to place a warm body in an empty office chair becomes the *Most Important Thing* the company does. Unfortunately, this nothing-else-matters rush to hire a replacement occurs too often, especially in small and mid-sized businesses.

Sure, someone might say, "We need to find someone who is a good fit for our company." Most employers, though, do not know what "a good fit" looks like, and, because they are concerned with the *Actual Most Important Thing*, the conversation doesn't progress much further.

I always say this: The second you think, *This is not necessarily the best person for the job, but I need a warm body right now,* is the second you have compromised your business or your department.

Think about it within your own company: When was the last time you thought strategically about the hiring and selection process or had formal training on how to interview and select the best possible employee? Have you even considered why a great employee would want to work for you?

What does that employee look like? Which of your current employees would you like to clone, and why? Lacking answers to these questions, most employers rely on finding a pool of candidates who are capable of adequacy, and then selecting the one with the shiniest personality.

Is this the best way to do it? I think not. As you are about to learn, ability is only one small piece of the picture, and personality can be ever so deceiving. In fact, most employers intuitively know that they are not using the best process for selecting employees. When we survey company principals, asking them to rate themselves on a scale of one to ten with respect to their level of confidence in hiring executives and managers, they consistently give us the same number: a six. This is the equivalent of a "D" grade.

Yet your workforce is the single key to your success. It's the most important component of customer satisfaction. It plays a significant part in determining your reputation among your industry, partners, vendors, and your community. And it is most likely the only true differentiator you have.

The truth is, no service that you provide, no widget that you manufacture, and no product that you sell is truly unique. Someone else is providing, selling, or manufacturing the same thing that you are. This might be a hard pill to swallow, but the truth is that, if you are a CPA, you aren't the only firm walking clients through audits and preparing tax statements. If you are an interior design firm, you aren't the only firm out there helping clients express their unique selves through residential design. And right after Uber came long, so too did Lyft.

But what about Apple? Surely Apple's products are unique, right? Even Apple wouldn't be as successful without the droves of people greeting you the minute you walk into an Apple store, or the people behind the scenes who have innovated over the years. (Steve Jobs was a controversial human, but he found and hired great employees and allowed them to innovate.).

Since nothing you manufacture, sell, or provide can truly be unique, you have to do it better than anyone else. At least ninety percent of the time, your team is the only true differentiator you can provide that makes you stand a shoulder above your competitors. It is the critical component in profitability and success.

Need proof that the team makes the difference? Take a look at Walmart versus Costco, Frontier Airlines versus Southwest Airlines, and a chain supermarket versus Trader Joe's. What's the difference?

Great employees.

I am always a bit tickled when a cashier at Vons glances down at my receipt and mutters indifferently, "Have a good day, um ... Mr. Swenson." Vons isn't the only culprit of the "look-at-the-receipt-so-you-can-call-the-customer-by-name" gimmick. The majority of major grocery store chains hire lackeys, give them a minimal amount of training, and then set them loose. Their lack of commitment to hiring people who are pleasant is apparent, particularly when they are compared to Trader Joe's.

Though Trader Joe's employees come in all shapes and sizes, they all "look" the same in one respect: Boy-oh-boy, are they pleasant to their shoppers! Your cashier might have fifteen nose rings and a sleeve of tattoos. He or she might be a pimply-faced teenager, a colorful hipster, a thirty-year-old soccer mom from the suburbs, or a seventy-year-old veteran wearing a lumbar brace. One thing is certain: Your cashier is pleasant, friendly, and helpful, and so are the stockers and the baggers and the managers. Above all, Trader Joe's employees are genuine about their helpfulness. They are friendly because they are naturally benevolent, gregarious people, not because they have to be.

Trader Joe's has pinpointed exactly what it wants in an employee, and hiring managers can spot the store's "type," regardless of whether a candidate walks into an interview wearing fifteen nose rings or tan Capri pants and a pastel polo from L.L. Bean.

Once you have identified the relevant attributes of an employee, they jump out, and you stop seeing all the irrelevant information. As much as the corporate officers of Vons might genuinely want you to have-a-good-day-Mister-Swenson, Vons does not know how to hire *employees* who genuinely want you to have a nice day.

Employees drive your customer service, which then impacts your community's buying decision, which then drives the behavior of upper management, which then drives the investors' decisions, which leads to share-holder satisfaction.

Your workforce, then, is the *Actual Most Important Thing*. (This section is focusing on *hiring* the right work-force, but the *Actual Most Important Thing* is not limited to

In the past, businesses used "time-to-hire" as a yardstick with which to measure their human resource department's success. This is a terrible yardstick. Employee longevity, turnover, and retention are far better indicators of a human resource department's ability to find and retain the best employees.

When you consider that hiring a great workforce is the *Actual Most Important Thing* you can do, you see how important it is to allow a job opening to percolate for a few weeks so that you can choose from the best pool of applicants. My clients know that the average time to hire a new employee is four weeks, and it is more often six weeks.

selection and hiring: It includes developing, managing, growing, and retaining employees.)

Yet too many employers are hiring employers based on a hurried and rash process that most likely consists of reviewing résumés and asking a few stock interview questions before sticking with "gut feel" and offering a candidate an opportunity to drive the reputation of your firm up or down. .

Consider the standard interview. It probably sounds something like this:

Int: *Tell me about your work experience.*

Jeff: I worked in Information Technology for four years at XYZ Company. Then I got promoted to IT manager.

Int: *Why are you looking for a new job?*
Jeff: I'm looking to make more money and work for a growing company.

Int: *What are your biggest strengths?*
Jeff: I'm a hard worker, detail-oriented, and I like working with people.

Int: *What are your biggest weaknesses?*
Jeff: I'm not very good at multi-tasking; I like to focus on one project at a time and get it just right. There really isn't room for any mistakes when you're working in IT.

The interviewer got answers, but those answers are not particularly illustrative of what can differentiate this candidate from any other candidate. The best interviewers, the ones using the Five A's, have the tools to ask follow-up questions that paint a bigger picture of the candidate.

Unfortunately, this interviewer was too focused on asking the next question on the checklist to consider the candidate's answers and what they mean. Ultimately, this interviewer probably ended up with a slew of candidates who all gave similarly acceptable answers, so the interviewer hired an employee based on most impressive résumé and personality.

Managers who understand the Five A's know how to determine which answers beg follow-up questions. After all, to get and keep great employees, you must ask different questions of different people, depending on the job you are trying to fill and the culture you are trying to create. Interviewers trained in the Five A's know that they should never use a standard checklist of questions to guide the interview; they should use the candidate's answers as a springboard for asking other questions!

Simply put, the Five A's focus on finding that great potential hire—the one who will most fit with your company's culture. After interviewing more than five thousand job candidates over the course of my career, the CEO of a bank asked me a simple question about hiring. I didn't have a good answer.

"What do you look for in a potential employee?" he asked me.

I have great intuition. No one hires better than I do. Yet, even after a career of conducting thousands of interviews and making hundreds of hiring decisions, I was caught off guard. I didn't have a concrete answer for him.

The next day, I had lunch with my principal business partner, Tony Rose. To know Tony is to know that he loves process. When I relayed my dismay about an inability to answer what should have been an innocuous question, Tony challenged me right then and there to identify what attributes are necessary for a person to be a great employee: What does "fit" really mean? Fortunately, the table at the restaurant was covered in paper, so I had an accessible scratch pad. I wrote down four traits right then and there (and was pleased that they all started with an A). After some reflection, I identified the fifth A the following day.

What used to be my intuition is now my intentional process. I've tested the Five A's on hundreds of candidates and employees: My clients will attest that a "great hire" will always score well in all Five A's, whether the position is blue collar, white collar, or some other collar entirely.

Too many interviewers pay attention to personality and résumé alone. This is the wrong move. A good personality and impressive résumé alone cannot determine whether an employee will fit, and by the end of this book, you will have downgraded them to the bottom of the list. The trick is defining what a "fit" looks like in terms of your company's unique values and culture. The Five A's focuses first on asking interview questions, then using management techniques to find a great fit, and finally developing these employees to become even better.

Here is what an interview with Jeff might look like under the purview of someone trained in the Five A's:

Int: *Tell me about your work experience.*

Jeff: I worked in Information Technology for four years at XYZ Company. Then I got promoted to IT manager.

Int: *Why did you get promoted? What specifically did you do?*

Jeff: Well, several of our employees said we needed a stronger social media presence, so I developed a business plan to integrate all of our social media platforms automatically, and then I got approval to put that on our corporate website. We won two International Awards because of it.

Int: *Why are you looking for a new job?*

Jeff: I'm looking to make more money and work for a growing company.

Int: *With all of the success you had at XYZ, why don't you just ask your boss for more money?*

Jeff: I have a new boss, and she is cutting back on expenses, so I don't think she would be supportive of my getting a raise.

Int: *I'm not sure I believe you. Sometimes, companies that are cutting costs will still work hard to keep their key employees. What gives you the impression that she won't be supportive of your getting a raise? Did you ask her directly? Or is there something you aren't telling me?*

Jeff: She's relatively new and, to be honest, I am not sure our personalities click. The corporate culture has changed since she came on board, so I guess it is probably time for me to move on anyway and find a company that is more suited to my personality.

Int: *How did the culture change? Give me an example.*

Jeff: It became much more uptight. The systems seemed bureaucratic. For instance, before she came on board, management was relaxed about schedules. We weren't punching time cards and getting written up for being a few minutes late. As long as we put in the hours and got the work done, the managers were happy. My new boss is a stickler on time cards. That feels restrictive to me and not very personal.

Int: *You mentioned getting written up. If I called your boss and asked her if you had ever been written up, what would she say?*

Jeff: She would say that I've been written up for

being late. I have three-year-old twin boys. Some mornings are tough. I usually make it to work on time, but there was one morning when my kids were really acting out, and I wound up arriving at 8:07 instead of 8:00 a.m.

Int: *What is it about our company that wants to make you work here?*

Jeff: This position gives me more responsibility and more money. And I understand you're in a growth mode.

Int: *We'll eventually do cost-cutting here as well. What will you do when that happens?*

Jeff: I'm not sure.

Int: *I need a better answer than that.*

Jeff: It would depend on when that occurred. Let's say that you hired me, I worked really hard but never advanced, and then you did cost-cutting. I suppose I would start looking for another job. But if you hired me, I worked really hard, and I advanced over the years before the cost-cutting occurred, I would probably stay, particularly if the culture felt right. I just want to work at a job that feels like a good fit. If I'm not being recognized for my abilities, then maybe I'm not a great match, and I probably need to find a job else-where.

Int: *What would you say is more important to you: having more opportunity but greater risk, or having a steady job with a good but not great pay check?*

Jeff: I like opportunity, and I am not particularly risk-averse. In fact, I do not mind risk at all. Of course, I would prefer to be in a job with longevity, but I do like the opportunity to advance.

Int: *What are your biggest strengths?*

Jeff: I'm a hard worker, detail-oriented, and I like working with people.

Int: *You know, Jeff, every candidate says that he or she is a hard worker and detail-oriented. Frankly, the past ten candidates have said basically the same thing, and I'm getting tired of that answer. I need you to do better. Can you give me an answer that differentiates you from everyone else applying for this job?*

(Yes, I really am that tough on the people I interview! Asking tough questions during the interview makes managing a lot easier!)

Jeff: Well, I like to really see what's going on in a company and make recommendations that can improve our processes and systems. It is important that I am in an environment where I can innovate. I work hard, but I like to spend time thinking of ways we can be better.

Many of these questions are behavioral questions designed to get specific insight into Jeff's past. What is essential is that the interviewer is listening to the answer

While this section focuses primarily on the Five A's as they pertain to hiring new employees, you will learn later that the theories herein should be expanded and applied to current staff members as well. Good leaders constantly evaluate and re-evaluate their team. After all, people who were good employees five years ago might not be good employees in today's market.

Change has always been a constant, but today's world is moving faster than ever. If your employees are not adapting to the speed of change, they will become obsolete. This is not a trend or a fad; it is a structural and fundamental change in the global business world.

Likewise, if a business does not rapidly adapt to change, it will become obsolete or insignificant when compared to companies who can adapt.

and deciding whether that answer needs to be illustrated with more color or detail via a follow-up question. The follow-up questions depend on the person, the position, and the corporate culture. They are not and cannot be written in stone, and they can be identified only with a firm understanding of the Five A's and how they fit into a specific corporate environment. Listening—the key to effective communication—is the single most important thing an interviewer can do, followed closely by figuring out what needs to be asked next.

The first interview with Jeff reflects the information that an amateur interviewer would have extracted— which is, not much. Most interviewers focus so much on asking the next question that they do not listen to the candidates' answers, so they cannot prepare good follow-up questions. The essential information can be discovered only when an interviewer can dig deeply by asking follow-up questions.

A trained and experienced interviewer will find a way to uncover the true motivations of a candidate, whereas a typical interviewer will simply go through a list of standard questions, which means he or she will receive nothing but standard answers. Such an interviewer will never get the information necessary to make an excellent hiring decision.

And, making matters worse, most employers do not know what to look for when hiring. Great employees have five distinct traits, but most employers look for only one of them—and it's the wrong one! This highly sought-after but not-so-important trait is the only one that the employee can acquire *after* being hired. It is the only trait that should not be a deal-breaker, and yet it is consistently the only trait employers seek out, while they ignore four other traits that should be a make-or-break deal.

Hiring great employees requires you to take a deep breath and slow down so that you can find the right person—especially when you are in a hurry. Only when you have your wits about you will you make the calm, rational decisions that allow you to hire great employees—people who score A's in all five of the A categories, and people who require much less management than those who are poorly suited for your company.

Fortunately, after reading this book, you will have a simple, focused, and customized process for interviewing, hiring, and then managing employees who are ideally suited for their jobs and your firm. Most importantly, you will know what you are looking for, and that is half of the solution.

By reading this book and applying the principles of the Five A's to your hiring, managing, and disciplinary practices, you will know what you are looking for, which makes it easy to sift through the rubbish. You will experience a happier, healthier, and wealthier business. You will have executives who can focus on the core business instead of being distracted by unhappy, mediocre employees. You will have employees who are properly aligned with your culture and who can focus on that which is truly important to your success. As your turnover decreases, your customer service will improve. You will enjoy genuinely engaged employees, who are therefore engaging successfully with your end-user. Profits will increase as new customers are attracted to your business and existing customers remain loyal to your brand.

The Five A's work in any profession in any industry. I have used this process to hire pool cleaners and attorneys, to evaluate assistants and partners, to reward the people who are lifting a company up, and to eliminate the people who are dragging a company down.

By implementing the Five A's, you'll have fewer headaches, legal issues, and non-productive drama in your workplace. My experience is that happy, engaged employees do not complain, they do not file lawsuits, and they do not make workers' compensation claims. Beyond that, happy and engaged employees are significantly more productive than disengaged employees.

And here's the good news: It is not even that hard to dramatically improve your workforce and transform the way you hire and manage employees, nor is it expensive.

It just takes understanding what a great employee looks like and having the courage to hire and fire accordingly.

With this system, you will never feel rushed or ill prepared, even if you do need to fill a seat with the urgency you believe you must have.

PART 2

USING THE FIVE A'S TO HIRE EMPLOYEES

In an interview with *Business Insiders,* Tony Hsieh, CEO of Zappos, said that bad hires have cost Zappos "well over $100 million." The U.S. Department estimates it at thirty percent of an employee's first-year salary. Other studies say the cost is as high as seventy-five percent of that employee's annual salary.

If you have ever hired someone who was a disaster, you know that bad hires can suck money from your bottom line in more ways than one:

- Underperforming employees fail to produce the proper quality and/or quantity of work;

- Bad hires generally do not work well with other employees, thus lowering morale (and therefore production and collaborative byproducts);

- They have a negative attitude that requires excessive managing;

- Underperforming employees have immediate attendance problems;

- Customers complain when employees seem untrained or incompetent;

- They fail to meet deadlines.

Hiring someone usually happens quickly—too quickly. A person's true colors are then seen afterward, when he or she is being managed. And by then, the problem is often too late to correct without termination. Bad hires can be managed in a variety of different ways, but they will still be bad hires. Indeed, studies show managers spend an average of seventeen percent of their time dealing with issues related to underperforming employees.

That means that employees who are failing to meet expectations are eating almost one whole day of your time every single week.

That's not the only cost of a bad hire. The price tag includes costs associated with lower productivity; time for recruiting, hiring, and training replacements; the negative impact on employee morale and clients; and the inevitable legal issues that arise.

And this is just the average cost.

And what about the stress? No one really enjoys disciplining or terminating underperforming employees (at least no one with a heart). Most leaders dread those conversations. This is why a rigorous hiring process is so critical: The more time you spend in the hiring process, the less likely you are to have a failed employee. Have you ever tried to rehabilitate a mediocre employee? Without knowing the fine details, I know that this process took longer than it would have taken to hire a great employee in the first place. I also know the rehabilitation did not ultimately work.

Whereas managing great employees using the Five

A's can be engaging, managing employees becomes nightmarish when the manager must assume the role of the disappointed parent of an out-of-control teenager.

All this leads up to the employee's inevitable termination. Termination is almost always an awful situation to address, one that is postponed by even the most proactive executives. Most of the time, terminations are handled as poorly as hiring, which can lead to legal issues down the road.

And to be sure, the "end" of the employment process always happens. The lifespan of an employer-employee relationship always looks the same:

Hiring ⟶ Management ⟶ Dissolution

So in hiring, age-old planning advice still remains: Start with the end in mind. Do you want to terminate the employee during an ugly, awkward meeting in your office? Do you want the employee to scream obscenities as he or she is escorted out the door by security?

The best-case scenario, then, is to start with this specific end in mind: The employee is perfectly suited for the position, meets and exceeds expectations, and retires or quits after serving the company enthusiastically for as long as she or he is needed. When the employee leaves, you wonder how you will ever find anyone to fill his or her shoes.

To enjoy this sort of fairy-tale ending, or anything that comes close, you must know the type of person you want to hire before you begin to evaluate your candidates. This seems obvious, but it isn't.

Virtually all managers who interview candidates ask questions based on the candidates' résumé and

It's not enough that a person can do a job; the person has to do the job, do it well, and know how to adjust so that he or she can do the job in ten years. Today's great employee isn't necessarily tomorrow's great employee.

Think of it like this: I breezed through high school without studying, and I received high marks. My sister studied hard to receive equally high marks. In high school, I was considered the smarter one—good grades came more easily.

By the time college rolled around, my performance was lacking when compared to that of my sister. She knew how to study! She was better prepared for the future.

While I was a "high performer" in high school, my sister demonstrated high potential.

The same should be required of your employees. Do they have the aptitude and the agility to do what it takes when the world changes?

Are they a high performer or have a high potential? There's a big difference.

skills-sets. But given the dismal success that most hiring managers have, it's obvious that the question should not be "Can they do the job?" but "Can they do the job and flourish within our culture—not only today, but also in the future?"

In the coming chapters, you will learn why hiring

with the end in mind by applying the Five A's allows you to create a culture of employees who are much, much more effectively managed. Then, in Part II, we will take a look at how to manage these A-Player champions once they are on your team.

THE FIRST "A"

ABILITY

Ability—or competency—is generally defined as a person's capacity to complete a task properly. This is the sole attribute most hiring managers use to determine whether to hire a candidate. It's also the sole purpose of a candidate's résumé, which is meant to indicate that a person is capable of doing a job.

In fact, ascertaining ability can be boiled down to a simple question: *Can this person do the job?* Experience, education, specialized training, certification, and qualifications are the biggest indicators of a person's ability. To be sure, ability is rightfully the first thing employers should assess when hiring a potential employee. It is, after all, the only tangible criterion.

Testing a person's ability is simple: Need a bookkeeper? Just hand someone a general ledger and say, "Tell me what this means."

The mistake that most employers and hiring managers make, though, is to place ability on a pedestal, as if it is not only the first thing, but the only thing. Overriding a person's ability is the fact that employers will not be able to manage a bad attitude, an employee who cannot adapt, or an unwillingness to learn and grow.

Because ability *can* be managed, employers must consider it as a starting point, but one that is incomplete and possibly even the least important quality of all. After all, an employee with a lower level of proficiency, but a high level of aptitude, can learn to become more capable. His or her abilities can increase with time, experience, and training.

Of course, most employers do not want to bother with all that training. They want employees to jump on board with minimal training and supervisorial guidance, so they look for the most experienced candidate, the one who provides the best indication of abilities on a résumé. With all due respect, this is an easy but ineffectual way out of managing. Sure, it would be nice to snap a finger and have a new employee up-and-running, but managing and leading a team take time, dedication, and devotion. It requires spending your own time training new employees regardless of their so-called experience.

I have a client who judges the effectiveness of an employee by how little the employee approaches him with questions or issues. If he has a mantra, it is "Don't bother me."

Yet managing people is all about being bothered, being accessible, and being helpful to a team.

What if an employee is one-hundred-percent capable of doing a job, never "bothers" you, and looks great on paper, but destined to sue your company one day because of his or her bad attitude and unacceptable values? Surely that headache is worth avoiding! You would probably be better off with an employee who is only sixty or seventy percent capable but who displays a higher level of "proficiency" in all the other intangibles. Indeed, the cost and time of training this candidate are nominal when considering the promise of grooming an employee who is a highly successful long-term hire—an employee whose ending at your company will more likely resemble that fairy-tale ending painted at the beginning of the previous chapter.

I call this the "Sixty Percent Rule," meaning that your

Many businesses prefer or even insist on an employee with a college degree, or especially a degree in a specific field. But experience usually trumps education. Take someone with a bachelor's degree in English, but who spends fifteen years in sales, marketing, training, and human resources. If you are looking to hire that person, how important is his degree in English?

Not very. Except for a few specialty careers, experience is usually a much more useful indicator of ability than education. If you are hiring a car mechanic, you don't need someone with a Ph.D., but you do need to look for someone who has past experience or qualifications that indicate his or her ability to understand the basics of car engines.

A close high school and college friend, for instance, started as an engineer, but became unhappy in this industry, so she quit and joined the hospitality industry. She is now a successful entrepreneur, who owns and operates a culinary academy in Northern California. I doubt very seriously if the bank saw her engineering degree as an obstacle. The bank did not need her to have a degree in hospitality so long as she had passion, acumen, and the ability to get and maintain customers. She got her start based on the latter factors.

search for a candidate must start by narrowing your applicants down to those who have at least sixty percent of the abilities you need. Ability is such a small part of what makes an employee great; the intangibles will make or break an employee. And because ability is the only one that can be managed, employers would be wiser to hire people because of all those other intangibles, which cannot be managed, which cannot be changed, and which cannot be overcome.

So yes, the search must start with ability. It is the first A. You would be a fool to search for an attorney in a roomful of engineers. If you are hiring an attorney, it's pretty important that the person you hire has a Juris Doctorate in law. This is a minimal qualification. It must be met. And let's face it: The first chance we have to evaluate a candidate comes normally when reading his or her résumé, which is packed with information about experience, ability, and the self-serving, self-identified (and probably meaningless) descriptors such as "hard worker, devout, self-starter."

But what about all those other qualifications? Once you review a résumé for minimal qualifications, shouldn't you spend the rest of your time making sure the employee is actually a good fit?

I'll give you the answer: Yes!

If you would prefer a candidate with trial experience, you can and should put this preference aside for *the right candidate* who can be given trial experience at your firm. If you are hiring a forklift operator and prefer saw machine experience, you should consider that you can train *the right candidate* to operate a saw machine.

Not long ago, I helped a client fill a payroll/HR director position that was unexpectedly left vacant. The CFO wanted someone who was trained in payroll.

"No one here knows how to do payroll!" he shouted at me when I told him that payroll experience was the least of his concerns.

I was far more concerned about hiring an employee who understood the nuances of human resources. Training someone to understand HR issues is impossible. A great HR person is intuitive, empathic, and can seemingly predict the future—not to mention that the position requires an employee who has innate interpersonal communication skills.

I argued that an employee who knew how to process payroll wasn't necessarily going to make it past Day One of a human resources issue.

"You need to hire a temp who can process payroll for the next month or two," I suggested. "Then let's find someone who understands the basic concepts of payroll but might need some training, but who can definitely take direction, learn quickly, and work with all levels of employees," I argued.

I lost the fight. My client hired someone immediately based on payroll experience alone.

My client was sorely mistaken, and today his human resources department is in disarray because his payroll administrator lacks all the characteristics of a truly great human resources director.

The Rule of Sixty Percent

Hiring great employees today requires a perspective shift. Instead of fixating on making the transition easy so that the next six weeks of your life aren't bumpy, look forward to the next two to three years.

Most hiring managers focus solely on experience, to the detriment of all the other intangibles. Based on my experience, this happens for self-serving reasons: A hiring manager wants the employee up to speed as quickly as possible. Long is the list of times I have seen so-called "experienced" employees hired, only to ultimately fail because they don't align with the culture, they alienate fellow employees, or they irritate customers. I know many managers who spend up to half of their working hours interviewing, recruiting replacement employees, or counseling mediocre employees.

So if you can spend a couple of months managing a person's ability by training him or her, is it worth it to have an employee who has two, three, five, or ten years of headache-free employment?

The Rule of Sixty Percent operates under the premise that companies would be healthier if they hired employees who were a good fit but possibly less qualified than those who are highly qualified but not necessarily a great fit. It's the difference between someone who is a high performer (who can fill the gap today) and someone with high potential (who can still be filling the gap in five years).

The Rule of Sixty Percent works like this: Start by differentiating between minimal qualifications and pre-ferred qualifications. I know a bright, adaptive, optimistic bookkeeper who quit her job at a law firm to move across the country. She applied for a bookkeeping job at a major theatrical casting firm in Hollywood using a specialized software. My friend did not know this software. Her résumé was immediately kicked back for this one and only reason.

Don't do this! She could have learned the software in a weekend. And she would have gone on to be a star employee.

I've been in the management, human resources, and leadership game for twenty-five years now, and I have seen hundreds of employees who are able to do a job well—that is, assuming they never have to interact with another employee, employer, end user, vendor, or other human being in any capacity. I have also seen people who are tremendously capable today, but who will be unable to adapt to the employment needs of the future.

These intangibles will never be seen on a résumé, and

they might not be spotted in a standard interview either since candidates know how to prepare for all those general throw-away questions which most interviewers ask.

And just look at the list of tasks and duties that are found on job descriptions and performance reviews. Virtually everything is laser-focused on abilities. Employers rarely ask for information that indicates a person's alignment with a company's corporate mission, vision, values, and goals; there's nothing mentioned about the capability of the employee to adapt to rapid change or an evolving work culture; and there's rarely anything in a performance review or job description that mentions that *how* the job is done is equally as important as *getting* the job done.

The first cultural change in managing your workforce, therefore, is to drop the obsessive focus on competency. The next change is to heighten the importance of everything that happens after the résumé is approved. In short, once a person's résumé has been approved because it meets the minimal requirements, treat all applicants the same, regardless of their experience. In other words, you place the attorney *without* trial experience on exactly the same level as the attorney *with* trial experience; you place the forklift operator *without* saw machine experience on the same level as the forklift operator who can operate a saw machine.

My friend and the brilliant ethicist Michael Josephson, author of *The Best Is Yet to Come* and *Making Ethical Decisions,* argues that businesses should hire for character and train for skills.

Warren Buffett has a similar approach: "In looking for people to hire, you look for three qualities: integrity, intelligence, and energy. And if they don't have the first, the other two will kill you."

Both are right, but I would advance the theory that

neither is quite right enough: You need to hire for skill (or ability), yes, but character, integrity, intelligence, energy, and agility count for at least seventy-five percent of whether a person is a "good employee" or a "bad employee."

Just look at that bullet list on the behavioral- and performance-related issues related to bad hires. As a reminder, they are:

- Underperforming employees fail to produce the proper quality and/or quantity of work;

- Bad hires generally do not work well with other employees;

- They have a negative attitude;

- Underperforming employees have immediate attendance problems;

- Customers complain when employees seem untrained or incompetent;

- They fail to meet deadlines.

Only one of these issues can be effectively managed: the first one. It is no coincidence that the first one is also the only one that has anything to do with ability. No matter how great he or she might be, a manager will never change someone with a negative attitude, unacceptable customer service skills, or who works poorly with others. You cannot motivate someone who does not want to change.

So if you cannot manage for things such as attitude and ability to work well with others, you darn well better hire employees who can already manage these things on their own!

Over the next twelve months, one of my clients plans to hire four hundred people to fill relatively low-paid positions, many of which are slated for graveyard shifts. To fill all those vacancies, we are hiring three full-time recruiters who will work from home in three different locations, reporting to their manager via Skype conference calls.

Having some experience in recruiting is necessary, but it is hardly the most important part of the job. Finding recruiters who are self-managed and self-motivated is far more important. They need to be willing to leave their couch and drive to community colleges, and they must go knocking door to door, and they need to know how to use social media to recruit candidates.

The recruiters also must be able to talk to people at all different levels, from the college kids they are hiring to the executives who understand the company's corporate culture. Beyond all that, they must be great sales people who can convince college kids to take jobs working the graveyard shift.

Did I mention that this needs to happen quickly? We need to hire four hundred people *this year,* so the recruiters must be willing to work under pressure.

While experience in recruiting is necessary, it is only a tiny part of the equation. I would gladly take someone who met sixty percent of my preferred ability if I knew she would get up off the couch and work for eight or nine hours a day from home.

Ironically, the people most resistant to the Rule of Sixty Percent are the hiring partners at accounting and law firms — who are also the people who are most in the know about how a bad hire can impact a company's bottom line.

A law firm (and a client of mine) with about one hundred lawyers recently lost a senior associate whose abilities were so specialized and technical in nature that he was the only employee at the firm who was capable of doing his job. The partners found a replacement who was highly skilled and specialized in the legal field of work, but who struck me as anti-social and devoid of the personality traits necessary to get along in a culture that is casual and friendly.

Because I was alarmed by the number of different jobs — six — that he had held in the past eight years, I dug more deeply to discover why he experienced such extreme turnover. It bears noting that in today's culture, rapid turnover isn't necessarily a red flag. More than ever, today's employees want to feel career satisfaction, and they are expected and educated to leave a company that is clearly a bad fit. For instance, some employees will work hard for a company, but then they leave when they are offered a position with a company with a stronger commitment to corporate social responsibility.

However, I discovered that this particular candidate consistently quit his job because he didn't get along with his colleagues.

I advised my clients not to hire this candidate. The partners rebutted my opposition by arguing that they did not need someone who got along with their peers: They needed someone to turn out the work.

"It will be fine," one partner told me. "He will come to work, shut his door, and there won't be any problems."

This just is not feasible in today's workforce. People want to work collaboratively and interactively with clients, peers, and vendors.

Sure enough, the complaints started rolling in: He was rude or otherwise ignored associates and clerical staff. When it came time to work on mutual projects, partners discovered that he favored certain partners over

The first rule of hiring is that there are no shortcuts. Doing it properly takes time and effort. My company helps our clients find dozens of candidates every year, and I review every submitted résumé personally. I also participate in the final interviews with executives, board members, and business owners. It's time-consuming, but the more you do it, the better you will be.

others. He was a loner: In a corporate office where senior associates often took their staff out to lunch, he would eat by himself in a corner of the break room.

Finally, he did not take criticism well, often overreacting when anyone dared to question his conclusions.

His ultimate termination was unpleasant. He was surprised and upset. He took his one-month severance pay and, within a week, he had hired a lawyer to sue for wrongful termination. The company settled for a five-month buyout. Combined with his severance pay, he received half a year's salary.

Let's take a final look at the cost associated with a hire made solely on qualifications and so-called "ability":

- Recruiter fee for employee: $25,000

- Six-month buyout to avoid a lawsuit: $95,000

- Recruiter fee for replacement employee: $25,000

- Staff time necessary to terminate the former employee, plus time to interview, hire, and train the replacement: 100 hours.

Would it have cost this much to hire a better "fit" without the precise technical ability, and then spend a month or so training him or her?

I'll answer for you: No.

So if ability is the first of the Five A's, but certainly not the last, what *is* the right method for reviewing résumés?

Screening Résumés

First things first: If you are using an automated applicant-tracking program to screen your résumés, know that potentially great employees are being eliminated from the pool. These programs look for criteria based on job descriptions that are often impossible for any one person to meet perfectly, instead rejecting any candidate who does not meet every item on the exhaustive list of criteria submitted by hiring managers. This list is often much, much longer than it would be if a person were reviewing all the résumés, because hiring managers figure that if a computer is doing all the work, they might as well find their "dream candidate."

This system poses two problems: First, Peter Cappelli, a professor at the Wharton School of Business, argues that these programs make it almost impossible to hire a "good fit." Professor Cappelli says that applicant-tracking software eliminates great candidates, leaving many jobs unfulfilled for longer than necessary.

Perhaps more concerning is that a "dream candidate" often doesn't look perfect on paper. What if a candidate has met sixty or seventy percent of the job qualifications, and further possesses an aptitude for learning, a strong desire to work for your company, and has the ability to grow and adapt with you? The applicant-tracking will kick this person to the curb.

I like automated tracking systems for handling the logistics of résumé submission and the filtering process, but I am not yet ready to turn over the responsibility of *selection* to a software program.

When a client has a job opening, I personally review every résumé that comes into the office—and I suggest that you do the same. This often means that I receive two or three hundred résumés. I believe that hiring is so important that I always insist on being the first reviewer, though I often let an associate review the résumés later and conduct initial telephone or Skype interviews.

Yes, I handle it the "old school" way, which takes a significant amount of my time. I argue that this is time well spent. Jack Welch, former CEO of General Electric, said that there can be no more important thing in business than whom you hire.

I agree: After all, we are talking about the future of your department, division, or business. You can't afford to make mistakes, whether you are a small business or large.

Being the first reviewer also allows me to see an overview of the résumé pool. Are the right kinds of people applying? If the pool of candidates does not reflect what I want, I might need to go back to the drawing board and rewrite the job description. In other words, I need to know whether I am hiring the cream of the crud or the best possible person for the job.

One of my clients with a job opening received a set of applications that seemed mediocre. The human resources manager narrowed the pool to five people by reviewing the résumés and then conducting an initial phone screening. When she came to me with her "rec-

If you hear yourself, or another interviewer, saying that you "like" a candidate, be sure to ask yourself, or them, why. Too many employers are seduced by someone who charms them during an interview. You need to know why a person is a fit in your organization, and this extends far beyond whether you "like" the person.

ommendations," she said she just didn't know if there were any standouts.

Together, we approached the hiring committee and said, "If none of these five people stands out during the interview process, let's start over."

By getting a sense of the overall pool, you will know whether to move forward or go back to the drawing board. If reviewing applications seems like a major time suck, know this: I can pare one hundred résumés down to twenty within about ninety minutes. Here's what I do:

1. I use an applicant tracking system to accept résumés. First, I scan them for minimal requirements. This is where ability and experience come into play, and it is usually the last time I consider ability as a component in a hiring decision. For an HR position, the minimal requirements might be as follows: a college degree, ten years of experience, and a certificate in HR.

   About four out of every ten résumés will fail to meet the minimal standards.

2. While scanning a résumé, I make note of anything that jumps out:

- Perhaps the candidate has worked at a company with a particularly strong training program.

- Perhaps the candidate's objective mirrors one of my objectives for my company.

- I like to interview people who attended community college. Perhaps an Ivy-Leaguer seems more impressive, but I can guarantee this about those individuals who went to community college: They are hungry and desirous. They *wanted* to go to college. They had a purpose. They have the right attitude, so they can probably learn to be capable.

- I also take a second look at people who served in the military. I recently had the pleasure of working with a thirty-year-old who did not graduate college, but who passed several high-level certification exams nonetheless. He is ten times more mature than any other thirty-year-old whom I know, and he has natural leadership skills that he learned in the armed forces. He can also take direction.

  People in the military know when to lead, and they know when to follow. They know what their job duties are, and they know when to delegate duties to more capable team members. They know when to jump in and help someone, and they know when to hold someone to a higher standard.

  Plus, they will call you "Sir" or "Ma'am," which is simply delightful.

How many candidates inflate their abilities on a résumé or during an interview? In my experience, at least seventy-five percent do so. This is why I always make this request during an interview: "Take me through your day yesterday from beginning to end."

This way, you can see whether the person's current job capabilities and responsibilities are aligned with your expectations. I cannot tell you how many times I have interviewed someone whose résumé indicated that he or she was a key employee, but when pressed for more information, the person turned out to be actually a low-level payroll clerk.

So ask tough questions, and follow them up with other tough questions. In the words of Mel Kleiman, if you interview tough, you can manage easy.

In this respect, I'm also looking for people who appear to more competent in some fashion than I. A lot of managers and employers think that if they surround themselves with inferiors, they will look better. That's not the case. An HR director at a client's firm surrounds herself with employees who are not nearly as good at their jobs as she is. She thought it would make her look better, but it brought her down. In the end, mistakes, oversights, and other inadequacies end up in the boss's hands and impact the boss's reputation.

On the other hand, if your employees work harder and they are industrious, you will have a reputation for running a company that hires great people. You will look good when your employees are competent.

R.H. Grant, the famous vice president and general

sales manager who is believed responsible for making Chevrolet the world's largest seller of cars, once said, "When you hire people that are smarter than you, you prove that you are smarter than they are."

I don't entirely agree with this sentiment, but it comes pretty darn close to reflecting my beliefs. Hiring great employees proves that you belong in your position as a manager.

It bears noting that people have all sorts of "smarts." Sure, people stand out if their résumés show qualifications that far exceed mine. So do people whose résumés indicate that they competed in professional or extreme sports. These people might not have the same certifications or industry knowledge that I have, but they probably have more endurance and agility. This stands out, and I want to consider them.

You want a team of people you can turn to when you are stuck. So have enough confidence in your own unique abilities that you can surround yourself with extraordinary people.

This is the extent of my review: 1) I look for minimal requirements, and 2) I look for people who stand out for some reason or another.

It takes me less than thirty seconds per résumé to decide whether to keep or toss the résumé. Remember, I am looking only for minimal requirements. (The real work starts when you call or Skype the candidate for an interview.) Out of every one hundred résumés, I'm left with about twenty candidates. Several years ago, when my wife was applying for jobs, I showed her my process—racing through résumé after résumé, and it horrified her. She assumed that employers would read every word of a résumé and cover letter. Nope. Most of us who have been doing this for years know what really matters. You shouldn't have to dig to find a stand-out résumé. A stand-out *stands out* — in much more than just ability.

That's why the rest of this book focuses on how to really find a "fit" for your company: by looking beyond ability to the four other traits of a great employee.

The Second "A"

AGILITY

Today's businesses succeed only by having fewer employees doing more. Agility, then, is a necessary characteristic, and it is the second A of a great employee.

This wasn't always the case: Up until about 1990, it was possible for a good employee to do one thing, and one thing well, and be successful for both himself and his employer. Today, though, processes and ideas change too frequently and quickly for a stiff, one-task employee.

Agile employees willingly take on new assignments, can stop in the middle of one task to help someone else with another task, and are capable of performing multiple tasks well. If a supervisor throws six things their way, agile employees figure out how to get them all done well.

And then there's the future: Agile employees aren't just great today. They will be great tomorrow, too. Just because a good employee can do the job today does not mean he or she can succeed four or five years down the road when my business looks fundamentally different.

So when hiring or promoting employees, ask yourself: *Can that person grow with me? Does that person have the capacity to change? Every time we change a process or a rule, does that employee whine and moan and complain and say, "But we always did it that way!" Or do they respond, "Okay, let me find a way of working on this."*

Can that person bounce back? Grow? Does he or she have potential?

The head of a small business service company confided in me that while his company experienced consistent growth over a fifteen-year period, it had hit the ceiling in terms of capacity. Though employee salaries had continued to grow, revenue was stagnant. No one could figure out how to increase revenue and profits by taking the business to the next level.

"We have the perfect group of employees for our clients' needs ten years ago," the principal told me sadly. Clients' expectations exceeded the ability of the employees to deliver in today's economy. Lacking more agile employees, the company was unable to bring new clients on board.

Don't let that be you. Hire with the future in mind. Promote not just on ability today, but on tomorrow's potential.

I work with a number of banks which are frequently involved in mergers and acquisitions. After a merger, the first thing the experts do is eliminate duplication. They identify employees who do the same thing, and then fire one of them. Consider this: If an employee could do just one thing well, and his counterpart could do three or four different tasks well, which one would you keep? If you are like me, you would keep the person who can be plugged into several spots.

In baseball, I have always admired the utility players. True, the home-run hitters are the big superstars, but utility players can play three or four positions. They may not get the fame of the home-run hitter, but every manager relies on the utility players to fill in during injuries or suspensions.

Those non-superstars are called "character guys," and it is no wonder. They add to the team in small ways, but because they are agile, they have can-do attitudes. (After

Much is made of the need for contemporary *companies* to be agile, but I'm talking about agile *employees*—though I'm sure that the more agile employees you have, the easier it is for your entire company to become agile.

Based on my many years of experience, I have a theory that the larger the company, the more difficult agility becomes. Large companies are generally more reluctant to implement quick changes and more likely to include several layers of decision-makers in any potential change.

Maybe for that reason, I find that employees who switch from large to small companies can usually adapt and flourish, whereas those who have worked for small companies only have a hard time adapting to a large-company vibe. Many find the many layers of the bureaucracy stifling and quickly tire of the corporate rigmarole.

all, they can do many different things.) As a byproduct, then, they have positive attitudes that infuse a locker room and a team with energy. Just as a negative person quickly spreads bad energy among co-workers, the agile can-do players can spread a genuine positive attitude.

While some teams do need the superstar home-run hitters, most teams will fare better if the majority of their members are utility players who can accommodate. Today, the person who cannot adapt quickly to change, or who resists new technology or ideas, is left behind.

Spotting the non-agile players is pretty simple. In 2000, it was the person who still did not have e-mail, or who rarely if ever sent an e-mail. There's always the curmudgeon — young or old — who, because of stubbornness or laziness, will not adapt to change.

Agility is even more critical for smaller companies. Employees at small companies need to wear many hats. If your employees refuse or are unable to move outside their job descriptions, you are in big trouble. A small company doesn't have specialists in every area; they have generalists who can do multiple tasks.

When change inevitably arrives, be it at a micro- or macro-level, you must have employees who find ways to adapt naturally. They are comfortable looking for solutions without having to ask, but they are confident enough to ask for help when they have exhausted their own resources.

Importantly, these employees are more likely to see the changes that are coming. Employees who can jump in and find solutions are more likely to be employees who are on the cutting edge of their industry. An employee who insists on sticking with tried-and-true methodologies will still be using DOS while the rest of us are tinkering around with the Apple Watch.

This go-with-the-flow and get-it-done attitude is the essence of agility, and it can almost *never* be managed into an employee. An employee who is uncomfortable with change will always be uncomfortable with change — unless he has a huge motivating reason to change. This is a deep-rooted and psychological mindset shift, and I can think of only one time when it was changed.

One of my favorite (and most aggravating) business colleagues, John, was in his sixties and resisted technology, especially e-mail. His computer was behind him, and usually off. John communicated by phone and by walking around the office because that was the way he had always done it. We could send him an e-mail, but there would be no way of knowing if he read it, because there would never be a response. No one expected that John would change.

Then he got engaged to a younger woman.

I sat with him one evening at a social event that his younger girlfriend could not attend. We were all sitting around a table chatting, but John was looking at his lap the entire time.

Finally, someone said, "John, are you—are you—*texting*?"

He sheepishly confirmed that yes, indeed, he was *texting*. Turns out, texting was his fiancée's preferred method of communication, and he had no choice but to adapt to her needs.

When John and his fiancée ended their engagement, guess what happened? John almost immediately reverted to his old ways. In all fairness, he still emails and texts occasionally, but not very well.

Agility and Your Management Team

Agility is a particularly important trait in managers. Managers carry the water for senior leadership. They are the face of what the Executive Tower wants do. So it stands to reason that they must walk the walk and talk the talk when it comes to agility and change.

Remember that managers are responsible for working with all different personality types. The ability to adjust and adapt management styles is part of a person's "Emotional Quotient," or EQ. If your managers can understand the people with whom they work, they will be much more successful leaders.

Many years ago, I was a group manager, overseeing ten other managers, one of whom was Luke. My boss did not like Luke; on the other hand, I thought that Luke was a stand-out. Luke's job was on the line, so I needed to show my boss why Luke was such an integral part of my team.

So I asked all ten of the managers on my team to meet with my boss and me. The first nine managers came in and reported on variables such as revenues, quotas, and this and that.

Then Luke came in (by my design, he was last). He went through his list of sales representatives.

"First up is Keith. Keith is usually a good performer, but his numbers dropped last year when he went through his divorce. We went to dinner a few months ago, and I encouraged him to start dating again. He took the advice and started dating again, and I'm noticing that as his mood improves, so do his numbers. I hear he has a pretty serious girlfriend, so I think his numbers will be up again next quarter.

"Next up is Joyce. Joyce is doing really well, and I noticed last quarter that she leased a nice car. I did a little research on the cost of leasing this car, and I realized that her monthly payment is probably a little bit out of her price range. I gave her some pointers on how she could work harder in a few areas to boost her commission, and her numbers improved by about fifteen percent. I think we will continue to see strong numbers from Joyce in the coming quarter."

Luke went through each of his representatives, point by point. He showed my boss that he really knew his employees, he understood them, and that he was agile enough to change his managing style for each team member. At the end of the day, my boss saw that Luke's emotional intelligence was off the charts, and he kept him on board.

Hiring managers with emotional intelligence means that you will have managers who understand people and can shift their own behaviors to get the best out of their subordinates. Have you ever known someone who has terrible interpersonal skills? Chances are, this person is rigid and cannot go with the flow during conversations — probably not a great treat for a manager.

Measuring Agility

Today, every employee has to adapt, move, and hit the curveballs. Employees who cannot do this will not be with your company in five years. Think of it like this: It was not too long ago that the biggest cities had only four or five ATMs; today, ninety percent of banking is done online. A decade ago, no one owned a smartphone; today, it is almost impossible to imagine conducting business without one. Businesses must adapt quickly, or they will perish. What will the world look like in five or ten years, when smartphones are considered dinosaur technology? People who are rigid will be unable to embrace all of these new discoveries and platforms for doing business.

Look at the United States Postal Service, which is almost entirely staffed by these people. With advances in other mail-delivery systems, the USPS is well on its way to becoming obsolete, as are its employees, who have very few, if any, transferrable skills.

Compare USPS employees to those who work for Disney. At Disney, even the CEO picks up trash. That's the person I want — that no-job-is-too-big-or-too-small person. Agile employees never pass the buck or refuse to do something that falls outside their job description. (In fact, in a job description, the last criterion should always be, "All other duties as assigned by management.")

Agile employees will pick up the trash, preferably without being asked. They will say, "I'll find a way to make that work."

They figure things out. They are problem-solvers, and their defining ability is an ability to do a bunch of different things well.

You can ask some questions during the interview process to measure a person's level of agility. Here are a couple of ways to measure agility during an interview:

- Establish this scenario with a potential hire: "Imagine that I asked you to come to work right away to help on a big project that could make or break the company. You have got a problem, though: Your five-year-old daughter's first dance recital is happening at the same time, and you have promised her you would attend. You aren't the kind of parent who would ever miss a recital. So what would you do?"

  An agile candidate will be able to think outside the box to offer some solutions so that he or she can still help with the "big project." Here is a great answer:

  "I would find a way to meet both of my obligations. Let's imagine that my role involves reviewing a document. I would let my employer know that I would work on the document from home before attending the dance recital. I would get as much done before the recital as possible. I might even slip into the lobby after my daughter's number was up and work on the document in the lobby. And after the recital ended, I would arrive at work as soon as possible to collaborate with anyone who needed to give me input."

  Here's a not-so-great answer:

"Well, that would be a hard choice to make, but ultimately my family comes first, so I would offer up all my apologies and help on the back-end."

The candidate is not wrong to put his or her family first, to apologize, and to help on the back-end. All of these are great values to have. The problem with this answer is that it lacks agility in and of itself. An agile candidate will think on his or her feet and come up with an answer that shows an ability to meet two seemingly conflicting obligations.

- Take the candidate through the office and introduce him or her to a senior partner or executive. (We will call the senior executive "Joe.") Then say to the candidate, "I need to make a quick phone call. Why don't you talk to Joe for a few minutes?"

Can the candidate handle the curveball, or does the candidate get tongue-tied and nervous?

- Ask this question: "Describe a time when you were put on a tight deadline during work, and you hit an obstacle that threatened your deadline."

> "The world is changing very fast. Big will not beat small anymore. It will be the fast beating the slow."
>
> —Rupert Murdoch

Remember, the best interviewers listen to a candidate's answer before responding with a follow-up question. The candidate's answer tells you what your next question should be.

That said, asking questions during an interview is not necessarily the best way to test a candidate's agility. Far better is seeing how your candidate will respond when thrown a curveball.

A colleague of mine told the story of her first interview out of college. She was a fresh college graduate with a degree in journalism, and she applied for a coveted job with a small but prestigious newspaper that covered the state legislature. When she met with the newspaper's managing editor during the interview process, she learned that she would be taking a writing test as part of the process. The test required her to read the "minutes" of a meeting and write a story about what happened during the meeting. She had thirty minutes to complete this task.

Then she got thrown a curveball. Ten minutes into the assignment, the entire network crashed. All the reporters in the newsroom lost their work. And my colleague was no exception.

She knew she was on the clock, though, and she knew the show must go on. She calmly picked up a pen and paper, and started writing. When the thirty minutes was up, she walked up to the managing editor and handed him a story. She had written so fast that the writing was barely legible. The paper was covered in arrows, markouts, and scribbles indicating her edits.

She was hired five minutes later. Even though the paper was physically messy, it was spot on. In a newsroom, people have to adapt, they have to move, and they have to hit the curveballs. And she did hit the curveball. Her writing was tight, energetic, and easy to follow. The network crash was a blessing in disguise: It ended up being the perfect opportunity for the employer to see just how adaptable she was.

One of my clients has a unique hiring process. In short, once the company has narrowed down its appli-

Steve Jobs always managed to find agile people and allowed them to innovate. He was a genius at many things, including creating a corporate culture that attracted people who were interested in changing the status quo. No one can ever accuse Apple of getting stuck. Consider the iPod: The first one was released in 2001. Today, it is almost obsolete, thanks to the iPhone.

cant pool to four or five candidates, the company calls all these candidates into the office for individual half-day meetings. The itinerary for the meeting includes three half-hour interviews with key managers, a tour by the director of human resources, and lunch with two peers. During the interviews, the tour, and lunch, all employees are evaluating the candidate's fit, and the day always involves a curveball. Perhaps the candidate will unexpectedly be left alone to chat with a key executive. Maybe an employee will interrupt the interview, allowing the interviewer to see just how quickly the candidate can jump back in and roll with the punches during interruptions.

You can also consider using a pre-hire assessment as a tool to understand a person's DNA, but remember that these assessments are just one tool. Never let it override your own observations. Just as you should ask a few other people to evaluate a candidate, an assessment is there to advise you, but always remember that *you* know your company's culture better than anyone, and that you are the final decision-maker.

I like to think of agility as the difference between a growth mindset and a fixed mindset. In the book *Mindset*, Carol S. Dweck explains that people with a growth mindset believe that they can develop their abilities by working on them. People with a fixed mindset believe just that: that their abilities are fixed traits.

Dweck points out that almost all successful people have a growth mindset. It is the only true way to learn. A person with a fixed mindset thinks *Why bother?* A person with a growth mindset asks, *How can I figure this out?*

Bonus Interview Questions That Might Indicate a Candidate's Agility

Discuss a time when you had to deal with major change in your work process or job duties. How did you prepare for the change? How did you respond in this situation?

Provide an example of a time when you had to take action and didn't have enough time to prepare as much as you would like. How did you adapt to this situation?

Describe a time when you had to complete a project in which there was very little direction. What are some of the issues you faced? How did you go about completing the project?

Tell me about a time when you had more work than you could handle. What steps did you take to ensure quality outcomes?

Everybody endures some stress in the workplace. Give a specific example of a stressful time at work. What caused the stress? What did you do to handle the stress?

Give a specific example of when you have had to handle multiple priorities. How did you meet all of your responsibilities?

Discuss a time when you had to deal with a major change in your work process or job duties. How did you prepare for the change? How did you respond in this situation?

Give a specific example of a time when a recommendation you made was rejected or criticized by others. How did you respond? What did you do next?

Problems and difficulties often arise unexpectedly in the workplace. Give a specific example of a problem situation and how you handled it.

Give an example of a time when you implemented a company initiative that you did not support. How did you handle this situation?

Tell about a time when you changed or altered a decision as a result of a different point of view. What occurred that made you re-evaluate the decision?

Describe a situation where you were faced with adversity. How did you handle the situation?

Tell me about a time when you changed your priorities to meet others' expectations.

Describe a time when you altered your behavior to fit the situation.

Tell me about a time when you had to change your point of view or your plans to take into account new information or changing priorities.

Describe a time when you had to adjust quickly to changes over which you had little control. How did the changes impact you?

In what ways has your current job changed since you started? How have you dealt with these changes? How did you feel about these changes?

Sometimes policies exist that we don't agree with. Tell me about the last time you disagreed with a new policy or procedure.

Tell me about two previous supervisors with different management styles. In what ways did you modify your behavior to respond to their style?

Tell me about the most difficult change you have had to make in your career. How did you manage the change?

Describe a time when you felt that a planned change was inappropriate. What did you do? What were the results?

Tell me about a time when you had to adapt to an uncomfortable situation.

Tell me about a time when you led a change effort.

Describe a change effort you were involved in that was not as successful as you or the organization would have liked.

Give me an example of a time when you had to adjust quickly to changes over which you had no control. What was the impact of the change on you?

Give me an example of a time when you helped a direct report, or other person in the organization accept change and make the necessary adjustments to move forward. What were the change/transition skills that you used?

Describe a situation where you, at first, resisted a change at work and later accepted it. What, specifically, changed your mind?

The Third "A"

ATTITUDE

Fire any employee who has a bad attitude. Period.

I wish I could end the chapter right here because attitude really is that important. No leadership technique available will transform a fundamentally negative person into a positive one. Besides, life is just too short to spend your time dealing with employees who are sucking your energy. I assure you that, when you fire that negative employee, his or her colleagues will thank you profusely.

While education, intelligence, and ability are important, an employee's drive is critical. Remarkable employees are driven by something deeper and more personal than just completing the job and taking home a paycheck. Something inside of them makes them want to be the best that they can be.

Never settle for employees who are less than excellent.

An employee's attitude — for good or ill — has a ripple effect throughout a company. A great attitude held by a remarkable employee can lift the spirits of your organization. And you probably know what happens when someone has a bad attitude: drama, rifts, coups, and lack of productivity.

I worked with a client to formulate this definition of a "good attitude," which my client uses to provide feedback during performance reviews:

We retain and reward employees who are courageous and fearless, relentlessly positive, and seek solutions rather than complain about problems. We value team players: people who are always willing to help a colleague in any way possible, whether it's offering to help carry a box to the car or serving as a sounding board for a customer service problem. At its core, a good attitude means that our employees have great communication skills (both listening and speaking), which are consistent, clear, thoughtful, positive, and effective.

What would fellow employees and customers and partners say about your attitude? Not everyone has a great attitude every day, but the employee who is significantly above expectations has that positive attitude a vast majority of the time, and is able to mask those few days when things aren't so great.

We need our employees to move out of their "comfort zone" and into "The Zone," where you become the person who knows and acts as if you are capable of taking us to the next level. We want and need for you to be a hero for us every day and always exhibit heroic, positive competence.

Heroic, positive competence: I like that. Employees with good attitudes have character. They can be trusted with expensive products, money, and clients. And they are optimistic and benevolent people. They're the people you want representing your company to clients, to vendors, and to the community.

This is why I suggest having a candidate's peers take him or her to lunch. When I help organizations create their hiring process, I always ask them to hand-select the two most positive, upbeat people on the team. If they could clone the attitude of two people, who would it be? I then have these people take the candidates to lunch and report back with answers to the following questions:

- Would they want to have a cocktail with that person?

- Will that person fit into the culture?

- Is this person going to fit in or tick people off?

- And of all the candidates for that position, which one had the best attitude?

The last thing you want is to hire the person who is going to plan a coup and create a rift in your office. If you have ever employed this person, you know that the fallout of office drama can be huge, sucking away hours and hours of your life and your company's productivity. You, as the employer, must decide what you want your culture to be, and then hire people who will fit well inside that culture.

Fortunately, it doesn't require too much time to identify the people who are most likely to fit in. They are nice to servers. They have thick skins. They interpret other people's behavior in a manner that is positive and benevolent. They help. They laugh. They smile, and they accommodate.

Of course, it's easy to say, "Yes! Of course attitude is important" when you are faced with a capable and positive person. But what happens when you meet "Dazzling Debbie Downer," an abrasive, rude, negative person, but who happens to be so unbelievably talented and qualified that it knocks your socks off?

Perhaps this person could blow the competition out of the water based on ability alone. Perhaps Dazzling

Debbie Downer is so ahead of the pack that she spots the trends before everyone else does. Perhaps she has the potential to land that client you've been trying to land for six months.

You're tempted to hire her, aren't you? Like most employers, you probably focus more on the *dazzle* than the *downer*.

Don't do it! Netflix calls these people "brilliant jerks," and says that if an employee behaves like a brilliant jerk, he or she will get a nice severance package. Author Mark Murphy calls them people "Talented Terrors."*

> *[Talented Terrors] are like emotional vampires that suck your lifeblood while fooling you into believing you have to take it because you can't live without their amazing skills.*
>
> *In one of our studies, we asked 6,241 employees to list characteristics that defined these great skills/lousy attitude folks. The top four responses were as follows, in order of importance:*
>
> - *Has a negative attitude*
>
> - *Stirs up trouble*
>
> - *Blames others*
>
> - *Lacks initiative*
>
> *As difficult as these folks are, many organizations*

---

* Murphy, M. (2011, December 9). Talented Terrors, "Bless Their Hearts," And Other Job Candidates You Should Avoid Like The Plague. Fast Company. Retrieved from http://www. fastcompany.com/1796678/talented-terrors-bless-their-hearts-and-other-job-candidates-you-should-avoid-plague

let them slide because on those occasions when they do decide to deliver some work, they can deliver excellent results. But make no mistake, Talented Terrors are low performers, and they may be the most frustrating kind there is. There's a strange power struggle that often occurs with highly skilled/poor attitude employees. They know you need them, and they will often test your limits to see just how much they can get away with. It's enough to make you pray for the delay of rush hour traffic in the morning, just so you can get a little more quiet time by yourself without all their drama and toxicity.

You have been there, haven't you? When you have a Talented Terror on your team, everyone is miserable. Even your best performers say, "Well, if that person can get away with that attitude, then so can I."

Slowly, everyone starts behaving a little like the Talented Terror. These people are like a bad rash that spreads.

You have experienced the employee who made you shudder. The employee who cost you hours and hours and hours of time in closed-door meetings. Does it ever turn out well?

I have been hiring and managing people for twenty-five years, and I can answer that question: It doesn't. These employees *never* adjust their attitudes. Not once in a quarter of a century have I seen a Talented Terror be rehabilitated.

Know without fail that these Talented Terrors will ruin your corporate culture. They will surely scrounge up a few sidekicks, and before you know it, you are paying a whole team of embittered little vermin who create a culture of distrust, back-stabbing, and gossip.

If given a choice between an employee with

"When most managers talk about hiring the 'right people,' they mean 'highly skilled people' who can do the tasks of the job. But when our research tracked 20,000 new hires, 46 percent of them failed within 18 months, and 89 percent of the time it was for attitudinal reasons and not skills. It's not that skills aren't important, but when the top predictor of a new hire's success or failure is dependent on attitude, then attitude is clearly what we need to be hiring for. By failure, we mean these folks got fired, received poor performance reviews, or were written up. The attitudinal deficits that doomed these failed hires included a lack of coachability, low levels of emotional intelligence, motivation, and temperament."

—Mark Murphy

mediocre talent but a heroic and optimistic attitude and an employee with oodles of talent and a bad attitude, I would hire the first one every single time.

She might not take your company to the next level, but the second one is guaranteed to smash it into the ground. People with a bad attitude cannot celebrate success. They cannot move toward success. To do so would be to operate against their fundamental nature.

When you finally fire that terrible, rash-spreading employee, everybody else starts sitting up a little straighter. They act a little better because they know you have taken action, and because they themselves feel cleaner without the rash.

And you will inevitably look back and ask, "Why did it take me so long to get rid of that person?"

It's important to note that there is a world of difference between an employee who has a bad attitude and an employee who challenges you. Employers should be enthusiastic about finding employees who aren't afraid to challenge the status quo. This is called agility and these are the employees who come up with great ideas to create better processes or products.

Author Jeff Haden writes, "Self-motivation often sprints from a desire to show that doubters are wrong. The kid without a college degree or the woman who was told she didn't have leadership potential possess a burning desire to prove other people wrong."

These people might at first be disguised as Debbie Downers, but they are far from it. They are Can-Doers. They question processes, and they question authority because they are always looking for new roads to success. They want to give an idea a chance, so they challenge people to make sure the idea has been looked at from all different angles.

Writes Haden, "Some people are rarely satisfied (I mean that in a good way) and they are constantly tinkering with something: reworking a timeframe, adjusting to a process, tweaking a workflow.

"Great employees follow processes. Remarkable employees find ways to make those processes even better, not only because they are expected to ... but because they just can't help it."

These people often have a great attitude, but not in an upbeat and Pollyanna way. They see possibility, so they question everything, and they continue to question it, even after months and years. In the right position, such a person can be an asset to your team because he or she will always be on the cutting-edge of new trends and developments, and thus can help you spearhead a new procedure for workflow.

Since attitude trumps ability, make sure your interviews are stacked with questions that elicit insight into a candidate's attitude. Here are a few ideas for starting the conversation, but remember that the true magic is in listening to the answers and asking follow-up questions:

- "When have you been dealt a raw deal at work?"

  When I ask this question, I don't let the person off with the textbook answer of, "Well, this terrible thing happened, and I realized that I made a mistake that caused it to happen, so what I learned is how to change myself to make myself into a more wonderful employee."

  This is poppycock, rubbish, and trifling. When candidates say things like this, I let them know that it will not suffice. I really want to know about a time when the employee was wronged.

  An employee at one of my client's companies was passed over for a promotion during a year when she really should have been promoted. When she found out that another colleague had been promoted instead, she marched into her boss's office and said, "Why did you pass me over? I deserved that promotion."

  Her boss was shocked, and he struggled to give her an answer. The truth was: He promoted someone who wasn't quite as capable, but with whom he clicked a little better.

  At the end of the conversation, she said, "What I'm hearing is that you cannot give me a specific reason I was passed over. I would like to know that I will be promoted if I do X, Y, and Z over the next year. Can I get your word on that?"

Her boss agreed. Today, she is an executive at the same company.

She didn't quit. She didn't sulk (excessively). Even though it was unfair, she found a way to make it work. This is what a good attitude looks like.

- "What 'killer app' is on your phone?"

Asking offbeat questions has two results: First, it measures agility. Is the person flustered beyond comprehension, or can she answer the question? It also gives you a look into the person's attitude. When thrown an offbeat question, is the candidate rude, or does she take it in stride, laugh, and tell you that her favorite app is *Shazam*?

- "We have a number of well-qualified applicants for this position. Why do you feel we should hire you over everyone else?"

Bonus Interview Questions That Might Indicate a Candidate's Attitude

Note: These questions focus on communication because a person's communication skills are a strong indicator of his or her attitude. Communication is largely an observable behavior, so you can identify many communication traits during an interview. However, if the available position requires a substantial amount of written communication, I recommend asking candidates to provide examples of their work.

Give an example of a difficult or sensitive situation that required extensive communication.

Tell me about a time when you really had to pay attention to what somebody else was saying, actively seeking to understand his or her message.

Tell me about the most difficult or complex idea, situation, or process you have ever had to explain to someone. How did you explain it? Were you successful?

Describe a time when you had difficulty communicating your thoughts clearly to another person or group. What message were you trying to convey? Where did the difficulty lie? Did you end up getting your message across?

Give me an example of a time when you were able to successfully communicate with another person even when that individual personally may not have liked you.

Give me an example when you were able to successfully communicate with a person whom you personally did not like.

APTITUDE

Toss aside, for a moment, your own definition of "aptitude." I have heard a lot of them over the years, and while many of them include components of aptitude, all of them fail to grasp the true characteristics of a person who has aptitude. Aptitude is:

- The ability to learn and think critically;

- The desire and willingness to learn new things;

- The above two, combined with intelligence and intellectual curiosity;

- The above three, along with a talent for doing certain things.

A robot or a high-functioning monkey can follow step-by-step directions, "plug in," and perform. Today's employees need to evolve. They must have both the capability and desire to do more. When change inevitably unfolds, employees with aptitude are the ones leading the change.

As recently as the 1990s, employees did not need to evolve. My great-uncle was a clerk at a department store for thirty years. When I started in sales at AAA, half of my colleagues had been with AAA for thirty or more years. Certainly, banking was stable: ATMs were a rarity

I worked with a client to formulate this definition of aptitude, which my client uses to provide feedback during performance reviews:

We retain and reward employees who are aware of what is happening in our company and our industry. Are you an expert in your field? Do you understand your role as part of a bigger strategic picture? Closely tied to attitude, this category also means ability to take calculated risk and get in the trenches to gain the knowledge and aptitude that can be gained only through experiences—sometimes challenging, uncertain, and uncomfortable experiences. When there is a problem, a person with great aptitude finds a way and even discovers a new opportunity. Though it might be easier to simply say "no," a great employee finds a way to say "yes" or "let's see what we can do," whether dealing with a customer service complaint or a logistical challenge in the warehouse. A person's aptitude is developed through a combination of learning and experience.

and were considered by many to be a novelty without a chance of widespread success.

Long is the list of jobs from the 1960s that simply do not exist any longer. Today, technology is driving at such a frantic pace of change that many of today's jobs will not exist tomorrow. Compounding the inevitable job-extinction are mergers, takeovers, and the constant "doing more with less" that necessitate a workforce that is willing and able to learn new techniques, skills, technologies, and more.

The days of hiring an employee for a job, and then expecting him to do that job for thirty or forty years, are over. Even the idea of hiring someone to do the same thing for five years is virtually obsolete.

Understanding aptitude can help you hire and manage talent for the three- to five-year plan, meaning that you can hire someone who will be the employee you need not only today, but also five years from today — understanding and learning what is needed to succeed today, tomorrow, and beyond.

Critical Thinkers Wanted

Employees who can solve a problem without constantly running to a manager for a solution are the differentiators. They are the critical thinkers, and they are in short supply.

One of my clients, the vice president of strategy for a large corporation, oversaw about three hundred employees. She was looking to replace a good key employee who had been promoted to a different part of the company. We sat down and discussed the attributes she was looking for in a replacement: She mentioned ability to think quickly and make decisions. She wanted a person who would come to her not just with a problem, but also with two or three potential solutions. She knew she could not afford to hire anyone whose performance would come to a grinding halt if he or she hit an obstacle.

As I listened to her, I thought, *My gosh! She wants the anti-Charlie.*

Charlie was an employee who was driving her crazy. She was never able to articulate why she had such a problem with Charlie until she identified the attributes she wanted in a different employee. Charlie was a good worker. He showed up on time. He had been with the company for years, and he was as loyal as could be.

But he walked into her office three or four times a day with problems. He would analyze an issue to death. Charlie did good work, but the amount of energy Charlie's boss had to expend just to get those projects completed often wasn't worth the effort. Despite all his great intentions, Charlie simply was not a critical thinker, and he never would be.

Desire and Willingness to Learn New Things

Before I hire someone, I want proof that he or she is able to learn new things. I'm going to screen someone out of an interview if he or she spent only two minutes on my company's website doing research. I want people who want to learn, who are desperate to learn, and who get sucked into their research. These people never get tired of growing.

If a candidate has not done research on the company, I question his or her aptitude. Does the candidate want a job working for me, or does he just want a job?

Curious candidates will ask questions, and they will be prompted to ask follow-up questions based on your response. Their questions might often seem irrelevant, but do not dismiss them as such. When a candidate acts interested in a topic, pay attention. The candidate might be showing you that he or she has the desire to move forward with your company and has the ability to learn more.

One of my bank clients wanted to implement an employee survey, training, and development program immediately. I worked with the CEO and executive team to develop a fairly comprehensive training program over the course of a year. The program included skills and tactical training, all the way up to a leadership development program from various levels of management.

Four senior-level managers elected not to participate in any of the training, saying in effect that there wasn't much else they could learn. How depressing is that? Their knowledge banks were already so full—or so they thought—that nothing new was ever going to come their way.

These four employees have tremendous experience and ability, but how well will this attitude serve them in the banking industry, which is changing as rapidly as any other industry? If they lack a desire to learn new things, they will be unable to lead (or even follow) when change occurs.

The opportunity to learn is something an employee should always take advantage of. I told my client that, if I were in charge, those four employees would be looking elsewhere for jobs.

How many new things are going on in your industry? How many changes? How many mergers and acquisitions? When I'm working with an M&A client, the employees who remain at the company post-merger are those who are agile and have aptitude. They can grow along with the company, they are not going to complain every time there is a change, and they are going to learn the new systems. They are the real deal, and they are the people I want working for me.

Intelligence and Intellectual Curiosity

A person does not have to be smart to work for me, but I would prefer intelligence to the opposite. Smart people generally pick up on things more quickly, require less management intervention, and can act quickly and effectively when things go wrong.

One executive whom I know asks entry-level employees for their grade-point averages in college. I believe this information is irrelevant. Of course, hiring a smart person is desirable, but too much emphasis is placed on variables such as IQ and traditional grades. Remember that intelligence comes in many forms, and it is up to you to determine what kind of intelligence is necessary for the position you want to fill.

Howard Gardner, Harvard psychologist and author of *Multiple Intelligences*, correctly points out that our culture erroneously downplays all but verbal, linguistic, mathematical, and logical intelligences. In this country, we recognize people with verbal/linguistic or logical/mathematical skills as "smart." Gardner correctly notes that these are but two of the nine intelligences a person can have. His complete list is: verbal/linguistic, logical/mathematical, musical, visual/spatial, bodily/kinesthetic, intrapersonal, interpersonal, naturalist, and existentialist.

On this list, those people with verbal/linguistic intelligence are the ones most often considered "smart," and it is true that they usually shine in interviews. However, exercise caution when hiring a person with verbal/linguistic intelligence. Since these people are almost always labeled as "smart," employers usually assume they can do any job.

This is not always the case, though. My level of verbal/linguistic intelligence is high, and one of my clients always says that because I am articulate, I must be intelligent. I do not dissuade him from holding that opinion, but I challenge you to look carefully at candidates with verbal/linguistic intelligence. These people will probably breeze through any interview, but can they fill the actual job requirements? If the job requires the person to grasp logical concepts, be sure they also have logical intelligence.

Understanding that intelligence comes in many forms helps eliminate biases. As a culture, we favor people who are articulate and, to a lesser degree, who demonstrate great logical abilities. But an organization might need someone who can solve physical problems, or a person who can relate to other people.

(My business partner, Tony Rose, frequently says that his ideal entry-level accountant isn't the one with the 4.0 GPA from Harvard, but rather, the B+ student from a community college who had to work hard for his or her grades.)

Intellectual Curiosity

My belief is that if you are not learning, you are losing. It matters not how old you are or how much experience you have—you can always learn more. You cannot force people to learn. That desire must come from within, which is exactly why I want to be surrounded by people who share that intellectual curiosity.

A favorite client of mine is the CEO of a professional services firm in Texas. In his mid-sixties, he still attends conference and pays a great deal of money to participate in strategic leadership programs. He comes back from these events full of new ideas for his company. In fact, his ideas come so often and on such a large-scale that he often overwhelms his executive teams. One of his vice-presidents is also in his mid-sixties, but he thinks he has been there and done that. He is not interested in anything new. In fact, his solutions to workforce issues are straight out of the 1977 Management Playbook.

His ideas also never stick, while my client's ideas have turned the company around.

Bonus Interview Questions That Might Indicate a Candidate's Aptitude

Here are a few questions you might ask to help gauge a candidate's aptitude. Remember, this is just a starting point. Everyone wants a list of questions to ask during an interview, but no interview should ever be considered successful if the interviewer fails to deviate from the list. Your ability to find the right candidate is not based on the questions you ask, but rather on how you react to the answers you are given with additional follow-up questions:

What have you read recently that made an impression and how have you applied your new knowledge?

What is the difference between a good employee and an average one?

Of all your work experience, what has had the biggest impact on your career and what specific things did you gain from it?

Tell me about a time when you had to work on a project or task that you were dreading.

Give an example of something you've done in previous jobs that demonstrates your willingness to work hard.

Tell me about a challenging project you worked on.

Describe a time when you had to act with very little planning.

Sometimes people delay taking action on something. Describe a time when you saw other people in the organization who were not acting and you took it up on yourself to lead the effort.

Tell me about your career path and what you have done so far to accomplish it.

Give me an example of how you have taken control of your career.

Give me an example of a time when you knew you had outgrown a position and it was time to move on.

Tell me about your greatest career achievements. Why did you pick those examples?

Tell me about a time you felt "off track" in your career progress.

Tell me about a time when you turned down a good job.

THE FIFTH "A"

ALIGNMENT

The Fifth A was the hardest for me to identify, and it was the last that made it onto my list. I have come to believe, though, that alignment is more important than any of the other A's.

I came to this conclusion based on several experiences in my own business, as well as from my conversations with an important professional influence in my life, Michael Josephson.

It's pretty difficult to name any ethicist in the world who is more passionate than Michael. For years, I listened to his radio commentary called "Character Counts," and he became a business idol of mine. In 2009, by a small luck of fate, his non-profit organization became my client.

Michael and I just clicked. Someday, he and I will even finish that book we have been discussing.

When it comes to business decisions, one of his mottos is: "Hire for character and train for skills."

His motto is self-explanatory: Character is far more important than any skills an employee could bring to your table. I cannot think of a single more important trait an existing or potential employee could have than character. It means doing the right thing, even when doing the right thing is not the most convenient, the least expensive, or the easiest to do. Character means stopping at a traffic signal in the middle of nowhere even when no one is around for miles. A person with good character does the right thing, period.

Most businesses preach integrity and ethics as core values, claiming that they hire for those attributes. But in many cases, the truth does not match what they preach.

One well-known company identified as its core values the following:

- *Communication – We have an obligation to communicate.*

- *Respect – We treat others as we would like to be treated.*

- *Integrity – We work with customers and prospects openly, honestly, and sincerely.*

- *Excellence – We are satisfied with nothing less than the very best in everything we do.*

But that company—Enron—didn't really live those values, did it? Turns out that integrity wasn't a core value, though it looked very nice in its annual reports.

I experience the same ethical dilemma with many businesses which profess to value ethics and integrity, but then allow their top salespeople to cut corners, treat co-workers poorly, or break the rules because they bring so much in revenue to the company.

Either you value integrity or you don't. I personally have a solid line about integrity—nothing is worth taking action without integrity. I started my company at the age of forty, and I didn't have one client. I built that business one client at a time, with a lot of help along the way. To this day, I remain highly selective of service providers to which I'll refer my clients. Almost all of my clients need insurance brokers, payroll companies, or executive coaches, but I rarely give out referrals. You see,

I don't want my reputation hurt by referring anyone who is anything less than incredibly ethical.

We all make mistakes—that's the nature of life. I forgive mistakes, but I will not forgive unethical behavior. I am not a saint, and I do not lead a perfect life, but I try exceptionally hard to uphold standards which I believe are important. When I hire employees, then, I need them to be aligned with me in terms of my ethics.

Alignment means that you establish a culture in your business that is true to who you really are (or want to be), and then you make decisions that support that culture. It starts, as most things do, with your employees.

Do your employees mirror your values? When you hire, are you asking questions designed to elicit responses that help you understand their alignment with your values and mission?

About twenty percent of my clients are non-profit organizations (NPOs), which are mission-driven by nature. Employees working for NPOs are almost always aligned with the mission. (They had better be! No one is going to get rich working for an NPO.)

One of the most transformational business experiences I ever had came from working with a non-profit organization. The NPO provided after-school programs for kids in poor neighborhoods throughout Los Angeles. It had received a federal grant to replicate the program in Phoenix and San Diego, and I was brought in to identify the attributes needed in program directors in those cities.

So I started by interviewing the existing program directors in LA. I had a prepared list of questions, which included this one:

If you won $20 million in the lotto tomorrow, what would you do?

Four of the five said, with all sincerity, that they would

do something in the after-school care arena. I was really surprised. Those four were truly and sincerely aligned with the mission of their organization. They worked there because they wanted to, not because they had to. That story highlighted the important of aligning mission values with employees' values. (The fifth employee said she would take the money and move to Tahiti—an honest answer that most of us would give!)

Yet a mission-driven culture should not be reserved solely for NPOs. Many for-profit groups have designed and lived up to their missions that attract people with the same beliefs.

Patagonia, at its core, is a retailer of outdoors clothing. But to describe it thusly is to do it a huge disservice. The company passionately believes in protecting the environment and in corporate social responsibility. Its mission statement is:

Build the best product, cause no unnecessary harm, use business to inspire and implement solutions to the environmental crisis.

The company is dedicated to finding employees who share those passions. In interviews, candidates are asked what their values are, what environmental issues are present in their hometowns, and the causes for which they volunteer. Their workforce has subsequently become a model for other businesses. Patagonia must be doing something right: It gets hundreds, and even thousands, of résumés for each opening it has at its corporate headquarters in Ventura, California.

Another example of alignment comes from one of my business partners, Greg Snyder. Greg is a tax accountant, and I have heard him talk to many potential employees about why he loves tax accounting. His primary reason is because he can and has built lifetime relationships:

Alignment starts at the top, with executives who are truly committed to values. When Patagonia's founder Yvon Chouinard found that some of his products were damaging the environment, he found ways to become more environmentally friendly. When Chipotle realized that some of its suppliers were using GMO ingredients, it made changes and stocked its buffet with only non-GMO foods.

He attends his clients' weddings, the birthday parties of their children and grandchildren, and their funerals.

When asked by a potential client why she should hire him, I heard and will always remember Greg's answer: "Given time, I will care as much as you do about your business."

In a seemingly simple sentence, Greg has communicated quite a bit in terms of alignment.

First, the sentence is a differentiator in an industry that isn't easily differentiated. After all, tax preparation is the same anywhere; Greg differentiates himself by caring.

Then, the sentence requires a commitment from the prospective client: "I will care as much as you do." In other words, if you do not care, I will not care—and vice versa.

That is a brilliant way of determining alignment, on both sides. After hearing Greg's answer, I started using it with potential and existing clients. I have found that if CEOs or executives really care about factors such as talent management, leadership development, and culture alignment, I will have a successful relationship with them. But if the CEO is going through the motions only because he or she has to, the relationship will not be as successful.

You must know what your company is before you can find employees who are a good fit and are aligned with what you believe. Be honest with yourself and clearly define your mission and values and those of your company (or your department, if you're a manager). Only then will you be able to identify the attributes you are looking for in employees. Without knowing this, you cannot know whether a candidate's personal beliefs and work ethic are aligned with your company. And remember: Hiring, or retaining, an employee who holds competing values can threaten your corporate culture.

A company's culture is defined not only by cause-related values, but also by its "personality." For instance, one of the reasons I struck out on my own was because I chafed at corporate structures that demanded a coat-and-tie appearance every day. It was symbolic of a bigger problem: I didn't want anyone telling me what to do all the time, especially what to wear.

Earlier in my career, however, it was harder for me to figure that out. In the late 1990s, a recruiter offered me a job as a national sales manager making twice the amount of money I had been making. The recruiter gave few details about the company, saying only that it was an "online" company. I met with two of the principals in an office in Malibu. When I arrived, they were in shorts and flip-flops. I was wearing a suit and tie.

"I'm so sorry," I said. "I must have gotten the time wrong. I'll wait in my car until you are ready for me."

"No, no," said Bill, who was thirty-something. "We come straight to work at about 10:30 a.m. after surfing. This is how we always look."

Then I learned that they were in the "adult online industry."

I passed on the job: At the time, our goals did not align. I was unwilling to work for the "adult online industry" because it would not look good on a résumé. I wanted to wear a suit and tie, because that kind of job looked good on paper. I was interested in climbing the corporate ladder (or so I thought), so the opportunity just did not feel right.

If someone is used to and wants a restrictive and structured environment (think a corporate cubicle occupier), he or she will fall apart in a loosey-goosey atmosphere. And a person who values a flexible schedule will never fit in an eight-to-five job.

Similarly, features like dress and appearance are part of your culture and your personality. Casual dress codes are more than handbook policy: They are part of your culture.

Whether you know it or not, your company has a corporate culture. If you have not intentionally defined it, your customers and employees have already done it for you. Take a look at Glass Door, or Yelp! Google your company, and you will see that people are defining your culture.

Your Mission and Values

The process of defining corporate culture often includes mission, vision, and goals. Herein, mission is the umbrella category for defining any of the following:

- Your reason for existing (usually called a mission statement).

- The long-term goal for what you want your company to be (usually called a vision statement).

- The one- to three-year goals that you have for your company.

- How you choose to define your mission is irrelevant. What is important is that you have a vision or a goal that gets you out of bed in the morning — one that defines your company in such a way that it makes you feel passionate.

If you are blasé about the future of your own company, you will never find employees who are excited to work for you. They too will feel uninspired. In this way, you might be aligned with one another, but you will never move forward. At best, you will remain in the status quo.

Once you have identified a mission that excites you, broadcast it to your employees. It should be on your website, in every job description, and in every customer contact. Cutting-edge companies who really value culture create video or PowerPoint presentations for current and future employees.

Take a look at Netflix' corporate culture deck, which is on their company website. The deck has often been called one of the most important documents to ever come out of Silicon Valley. It has been one of the most impactful documents I have ever read, and it influences much of what I do in helping businesses (or divisions of businesses) identify and define their own corporate culture.

Your actual company values are illustrated not only by who gets rewarded, promoted, and fired, but also by whom you hire. When you hire someone, his or her personal values will either strengthen or corrupt the values of the people who come into contact with that person.

Is corporate social responsibility one of your values? I see firms having great success aligning their employees with their own values by giving two paid days off each year to every employee so the employees can donate this time to their favorite charity.

But remember: Values are things you *want* to do, not things you *have* to do, so adopt a program like this only if it excites you!

Another client of mine gave each of her low-level employees $400 to spend on something they would otherwise never treat themselves to. She asked them to come back and tell the rest of the team how they spent the money.

By doing this, she showed her employees that she cared about them, and it gave her insight into their values, which allowed her to better lead them.

One of my clients, a law firm, values team players. The principal partner of the firm hired an assistant, Janice, whom he thought was excellent. The trouble was, everyone around her hated her. She stepped on toes, never gave credit, and spent her off-time on Facebook while her colleagues were rushing to hit deadlines. This situation went on and on for several years. It eventually impacted firm morale; everyone except Janice was pitching in to help. Employees were e-mailing and calling me, begging me to talk to the principal partner.

That was not an easy conversation. She was terrific to him, but not anyone else.

He finally had no choice and fired her. On a personal level, he was devastated, and he admits that no one he has hired since has measured up to Janice's level of proficiency for his needs. Intrinsically, he knows he made the right choice: She was making everyone around her feel bitter and resentful.

He knew that if he wanted his corporate culture to be honored, he had to set the example. As long as Janice stayed on board, no one would believe that the company valued team players.

Of course, you don't have to believe that being a team player is important. A bank might want to hire relationship managers who are highly competitive. As long as managers bring in millions of dollars in deposits and loans, the bank might not care how well they work with other managers. Hiring employees who aren't team players might not be problematic for this bank.

The problems crop up when you say that you value one thing, while at the same time hiring, promoting, and rewarding people who do not manifest this value.

Here's a way to identify your own values and your existing corporate culture. Ask yourself these questions:

- *What do people think when they think of your company?* And by people, I mean your community, your vendors, your clients, your strategic partners, and your competitors.

- *What is the culture as your current employees define it and as your potential employees perceive it?* You can start the process of identifying your values by asking your employees this simple question: "Other than the money, why do you stay here?" This will tell you what you have naturally done to establish your environment.

Their responses will also help you identify a corporate culture that was built unintentionally. If you want to value team work, but your employees all say that they stay because they love the "crush 'em" attitude of their competitors/colleagues, you might have some work to do on changing your corporate values from the top down!

- *Why would a great employee want to work for you or stay working for you?* The best employees have jobs that they already like (which is one of the reasons I recommend that you keep job listings "open" for several weeks). If you cannot identify why a great employee would leave an existing job to work for your company, chances are, you will recruit people who are unemployed or who are disgruntled.

Alignment with Corporate Strategy

Taking time to understand your own corporate culture positions you to understand what your employees should be doing. Gaylen Nielsen is one of the co-authors of *Fake Work: Why People Are Working Harder Than Ever but Accomplishing Less, and How to Fix the Problem.* I heard him speak at a conference in Arizona in 2011 and subsequently followed up with him.

Nielsen and his co-author, Brent Peterson, posit with substantial research that "much of the hard work people do for their organization does little to link people to the strategies that are intended to help the organization achieve its goals."

Think about all the incredible to-do lists employees have. Are the lists just busy work, or do they really advance the overall mission, vision, values, goals and strategies of the business?

The authors discovered that roughly fifty percent of the work employees do "fails to advance the organizations' strategies." In other words, it is "fake work." Most of those employees work with great intentions; they just don't contribute to the bottom line

By understanding the goals and values of a business, employees can focus on what work they can do that does advance their strategies and goals.

The Aligned Candidate and Employee

There are people who want to move up the ladder as fast as possible. Do you want to hire these people? Can you offer this opportunity? Only when you have defined your own values and corporate culture can you begin to understand what a "good fit" looks like.

A great way to determine whether a candidate's values are aligned with yours is by including a peer lunch during the interview process. When I help my clients establish hiring processes, I suggest that the interview process take about four hours and include lunch with two people who would be peers of that candidate. A candidate will be more likely to open up and answer questions that are indicative of his or her values if he or she is at lunch with equals.

Since everyone wants a list of questions to measure alignment, I am including such a list, but my usual disclaimer exists. There is no panacea for hiring and retaining aligned employees; most of it is instinctive and based on experience. But I am sure about one thing: The questions you and your hiring team have been asking are not relevant to today's great employee.

Here are some new questions you and your team members can ask to get you started. Because alignment is so important, the list of questions is long. Find the ones that apply to your organization, and go from there:

- *"What's the most important lesson you learned from one of your parents?"*

  Everyone's values began by either accepting or dismissing his or her parents' values, so this will give you a glimpse into the person's value set.

- *"What company do you most admire? Why?"*

  A company such as Apple is hugely successful, makes a lot of money, and constantly innovates. A company such as Patagonia is dedicated to corporate social responsibility and has a culture in which employees thrive. At Costco, the CEO makes far less than most CEOs working for similar-sized companies. The employees make more than their counterparts in other retail warehouse businesses. I have worked with a bank client who will establish accounts only for businesses that are green.

  The answer to this question will tell you what kind of company your candidate or employee would likely flourish in.

- *"How do you think punctuality affects a company's culture? Do you prefer an environment where you show up on time, or where you show up whenever you want as long as you do the work?"*

  Punctuality is a deal-breaker for me, and I'm not alone. I do not have a long set of rules, but punctuality is on the list. Other companies—Netflix and Google are two of them—do not care about punctuality, but for me, being on time is not an option.

- *"On a scale of one to ten, how would you rate yourself on teamwork?"*

Then follow-up with: *"What makes you an X? What would it take to raise your score?"*

When Marissa Mayer became CEO of Yahoo, one of her first acts was banning employees from working at home.* "[P]eople are more productive when they're alone," she said, "but they're more collaborative and innovative when they're together. Some of the best ideas come from pulling two different ideas together."

I generally agree with this sentiment. Writers, philosophers, and bookkeepers can work alone most of the time, but most employees will be best served through collaboration.

- *"Describe a time when politics at work affected your job. How did you deal with it?"*

This tells you how much bureaucracy bothers a candidate. Top-heavy organizations will not be served well by a candidate who gets excessively affected by bureaucracy. Employers trying to avoid bureaucracy should avoid employees who incite politics.

---

* Tkaczyk, C . (2013, April 19). Marissa Mayer breaks her silence on Yahoo's telecommuting policy. *Fortune.* Retrieved from http://fortune.com/2013/04/19/marissa-mayer-breaks-her-silence-on-yahoos-telecommuting-policy/.

- *"Tell me what steps you took to go about learning how your current organization works."*

An employee who takes steps to learn how a company works is likely a team player. A candidate who already knows something about how your company works is even better—this shows aptitude and intellectual curiosity.

- *"Tell me about a time when someone came to you with a problem. What did you do?"*

The answer to this question will shine a light on how well the candidate solves problems and works with other people.

- *"Describe a time when you were able to establish rapport with a person whom others referred to as 'difficult.'"*

This is a particularly great question to ask candidates for a managerial role, but it is appropriate for anyone who might be working on a team. A candidate who can showcase an ability to get along with all sorts of personalities is adaptable and agile.

- *"Tell me about a time when you used your knowledge of the organization to get what you needed."*

Everyone knows that my client Timothy gets things done. If the lowest-level assistant's printer is broken and the tech department isn't responding, the assistant can march into Timothy's office and tell him that the tech department isn't responding to her request. Steam will rise from Timothy's ears, and he will march down the hall and scream at the head of tech.

Every employee knows this, but only some will use it to their advantage. Some employees will follow the chain of command, while others will go over the heads of four layers of managers, march into the president's office, and make things happen.

Depending on your organization, neither type of employee is necessarily right or wrong. It's a matter of what works best in your culture.

- *"Please explain to me the most effective way for optimizing your performance."*

I do not work well from home. I will always find something I would rather be doing than working. My most productive environment is a quiet office where I can occasionally interact with people. One of my colleagues believes that he is more productive when he dresses in a suit.

Knowing what makes the candidate ticks helps you decide whether his or her conditions for optimal performance fit into your workplace.

- *"Would you be happier at a job with a lot of upward mobility but little in the way of corporate social responsibility, or a job that has fewer opportunities for growth but is deeply committed to corporate social responsibility?"*

This is another way of saying, "Are you motivated by money?"

There is nothing wrong with hiring a person who is motivated by money. A sales associate whose salary is based primarily on commission damn well better be motivated by money. Just know that an employee who comes to you

A world of difference exists between a person with a good personality, and a person who is compatible (aligned). Rookie interviewers often hire people because they like them. They mistake good rapport for alignment. It's not the same thing. You might enjoy a candidate's sense of humor, his *joie de vie*, and his enthusiasm for origami, but is he aligned with your company's *values?* If he values money over corporate social responsibility, he will not fit into a Patagonia-type culture.

because of money will leave you if the money doesn't grow.

- *"Give me an example of a time when you realized that you were overburdened with work. What did you do? How did your action affect the situation?"*

We all get into situations where our backs are against the wall. The distinguishing factor is how people handle it. If I am overwhelmed, I tend to shut down because I do not know where to start. The other day, I had seventy-two things on my to-do list, so instead of picking one, I played Spider Solitaire for ten minutes when I arrived to work. This might seem like a terrible idea, but it allowed me to let go of my anxiety, and then I was able to hit the to-do list.

Having the insight to know how I personally react to being overwhelmed is rare. Most people do not recognize their own patterns. An employee who is introspective and agile will know what he or she does to handle excessive stress.

Full Disclosure

In addition to asking smart questions to elicit information about the candidate, disclose information about yourself. Remember, alignment is a two-way street.

When I hired my assistant, I told her a few things: "I want to let you know the things that drive me crazy. I have a hard time with people who are not punctual. I also want to let you know my flaws. I'll try to remember to thank you everyday, but I'm not sensitive all of the time. I am occasionally going to lose my temper. My tantrum will last about thirty seconds. If I am really upset, I will call you into my office to discuss things. Otherwise, you should ignore my tantrum the same way you might ignore a two-year-old's tantrum."

If you want to know whether you are aligned with someone, you must be honest with the details. In a long-term sustainable relationship, all the details become important. You don't want that rock-star new employee to quit because the job and the boss were not what the candidate expected.

Be Like Bill

In some ways, alignment is the hardest attribute to identify. To some degree, every candidate will tell you what you want to hear. This is where being able to listen and ask great follow-up questions is so imperative.

The only real way to build this skill is to practice. Your best shot at coming out of the gate strong is to tune everything else out.

Bill Clinton is known for making every person he spoke with feel as if he or she were the only person in the room. When you are interviewing a candidate, that candidate is the *Actual Most Important Thing.*

Care about what the candidates are saying. Replace thoughts such as, "I have to interview one hundred people and then finish one hundred things," with thoughts such as, "This is the most important thing I'm going to do today. This interview is essential to me."

Remember, no one cares as much as you care about your company or division. In this case, you cannot care about anything more than the person to whom you are talking.

PART 3

USING THE FIVE A'S TO MANAGE EMPLOYEES

During a leadership seminar I held recently in San Francisco, a participant raised his hand and asked a great question.

"Why isn't 'accountability' one of the Five A's? Or should it become the Sixth A?"

He had a solid point. Great employees hold themselves accountable. When businesses ask their employees for self-evaluations, 99 percent of great employees give themselves low scores. Why? Because across the board, in every industry from high-tech to manufacturing, great employees expect more of themselves, whereas bad employees vastly overestimate their self-worth. I have rarely seen an exception to that rule.

Accountability, after considerable reflection, is actually a subset of both alignment and attitude, and employees who are accountable are the ones who are easiest to manage.

If employers find and develop employees who are aligned with their mission, vision, values, and goals, they can expect to manage employees who expect more of themselves. A company that hires people with great attitudes will not need to spend time managing people who pass the buck and refuse to rise to the occasion.

A high-tech client of mine recently told me that he and the partners were working on Sundays. This particular company has a six-day workweek, and the client explained that the rank and file did not like working Saturdays: They preferred working on Sundays. This meant that all the partners who oversaw employees were required to work on Sundays, which was not their preference.

I was astonished, and I asked how the new schedule was working.

"We still missed some deadlines," he told me.

"What are you going to do about that?" I asked.

"What do you mean?" he said.

"People who miss deadlines do not get to choose what days they work. They do not get bonuses. They do not get raises. If you do not hire for accountability, and you have partners who are not holding the employees accountable, they have no downside. They have no consequence for inaction."

Accountability comes from within (attitude), but it also comes from your corporate culture (alignment). If people know that they can work the system and get away with anything, they will do it. They are going to miss deadlines. They will pass the buck. They will never be great team players willing to pick up the slack.

If you complain, or if your executives and managers complain about having employees who lack accountability, make sure those executive look directly in the mirror. Sure, it's great to hire for alignment and attitude, but when it comes to holding employees accountable, the first responsible party I look at is the management team. As a leader, you *must* hold people accountable.

I have a question that I frequently use when giving talks to CEO groups or organizations. Many managers wait until an annual performance review to give both positive and negative feedback. As such, the performance review becomes a crutch and excuse, rather than a positive way of developing employees and giving immediate feedback. So I ask my audience:

"If your kid screws up, are you going to wait for his annual performance review to mention it to him?"

Of course not. Accountability and feedback, either positive or negative, should be given instantly. This is how you begin to create a culture of accountability.

When it comes to managing employees, then, I challenge any business owner or CEO reading this book to simply sit down and: 1) rank his or her employees for each of the Five A's; and 2) rate each employee on a scale of one to five for each of the Five A's.

It really is as simple as understanding the Five A's, and then being willing to measure, terminate, train, or promote based on an honest assessment of each employee's ranking and rating on the Five A's.

THE PROBATIONARY PERIOD

This chapter applies to employees whom you have just hired, and it might be the most critical part of the intake of a new employee. Most employers give only lip service to this "probationary period," but it is largely imaginary. The new employee gets wrapped up in the daily life of the company, and before you know it, the probationary period has passed. Instead of putting the time and energy into an evaluation, you simply give the employee his or her next paycheck and continue along, business as usual.

Michael Josephson, the brilliant ethicist and one of the major influences in my life, has spoken frequently with me about the need to put teeth into the probationary period. When you realize just how important it is to have the right employee in the right position, you will understand how important it is to have an actual probationary period.

First, the act of probation sets the tone. When your new employee realizes that he or she is being evaluated, the employee starts with the end in mind. The employee knows: *I am here to do a job, and if I do not do that job, I will not be here.*

When your probationary period is largely a sham, you tell your employees that you do not follow through, that deadlines are not really deadlines, and that people do not mean what they say around here.

That's no way to lay the foundation for a successful, proactive team.

Using the Five A's, the three-month probationary period is real. We tell our employees that they will have weekly evaluations and meetings to discuss the Five A's, and then we carry through with this plan.

On Day Eighty-five, we approach that person's boss and ask, "If you had a choice, would you rehire this person based on what you now know?"

If the answer is "yes," we keep the employee and have a party. If the answer is "no," we let him or her go. And if the answer is "I don't know," we remind the employee's manager of two things:

1. "If you think the employee is going to improve, you are wrong."

    A new job is just like a new relationship— the person is on his or her best behavior in the first ninety days. If the manager is hoping the employee steps up his or her game, we remind that manager that this is not going to happen. Let the employee find employment elsewhere. In other words, don't look for adequacy. Make a plan to get rid of the bad hire and replace him or her with someone who can elevate the company.

2. "It's your job to know."

    If the manager doesn't know whether he or she would rehire the employee because he or she does not have enough information, we have a word with that manager. It's his or her job to manage and evaluate the employee.

Once the probationary period is over, we let the employee know that the weekly evaluations and meetings will stop, but his or her employment will technically be "on probation" for the rest of his or her career at your company. Every state except Montana has the concept of "at-will" employees, which means that employees can be fired at any point for any reason except those covered by the law (like discriminatory or whistle-blower laws), and they can quit at any point.

The point here is not to be harsh with a new hire, but to let the employee know that mediocrity will not be tolerated and that he or she is being asked to be a great employee. This sets a strong expectation and initiates all of your employees into your culture of holding people accountable.

CULTIVATION AND PERFORMANCE REVIEWS

I do not believe in performance reviews. In short, I believe the performance review is an outdated parochial system designed to treat everyone the same in a world where fair and equal are no longer the same thing. As mentioned earlier, managers use performance reviews as a crutch. Instead of having real-time conversations with their employees, managers decide to "store up" all their feedback and wait for the performance review, at which point they have either forgotten about it, or they no longer consider it a big enough deal to address.

When a manager holds employees accountable, the manager gives them feedback immediately. Think of it like this: Let's say that your son gets caught stealing candy from a store. Are you going to wait until your annual performance review to talk to him about this?

No. You are going to give him feedback immediately.

If you think your performance reviews are worthwhile, let me put them to the test with one question:

Call a key employee into your room—one who

reports to you daily. Ask that employee to tell you what one of the organization's specific goals is.

Can he or she do it?

I doubt it. Quick: Do you know what one of your employee's professional goals is, without asking?

I didn't think so.

Performance reviews are rarely motivational, almost always time-consuming, and mostly ineffective. Employers do not know how to conduct them, and employees spend a lot of time and anxiety worrying about the review, only to return to business as usual once the review is over.

That said, performance reviews can be helpful if they are done right, meaning that they communicate the following message to the employee: *We are committed to catching you doing things right all of the time.*

If you are going to use performance reviews, I suggest holding them often and making them a part of your culture, calling them "performance and cultivation previews." In this way, they stop being reviews of the past and start being previews of the future.

For a larger, more detailed explanation of a performance and cultivation preview I created for a client, see the Appendix.

SUMMARY

About ten years ago, at one of my seminars, I couldn't help but notice a man in the front row, furiously taking pages of notes. I figured he must be new to supervising or managing because he was so keenly interested in every word I was saying. When I found out he had already built a small empire of fourteen different businesses, I had to ask why he was so extraordinarily attentive.

"I have only one job," he told me. "That job is to hire the right people. If I hire the right people, I don't have to do anything else."

Red Auerbach, president of the Boston Celtics, famously said: "If you hire the wrong people, all the fancy management techniques in the world won't bail you out."

APPENDIX

UNIQUE HIRING PROCESS

When the Five A's are adopted, your entire process is impacted, from posting a job description to greeting the person you finally select to join your team. Here is a synopsis of a unique hiring process I helped one of my clients create. It includes:

1. Posting a Five A's job description.

2. Screening the initial résumés and narrowing the candidate pool.

3. Conducting a Skype screening and narrowing the pool down even further.

4. Conducting a first-level interview, narrowing the applicant pool down to four or five candidates.

5. Conducting the second-level (final) interview.

6. Compiling assessments and making a decision.

At each level, every team member involved in the process assesses the candidate's ability, agility, attitude, aptitude, and alignment. Let's take a look at each stage of the hiring process in detail.

1. Job Description Posting

Job descriptions typically consist of:

- A paragraph explaining the functions of the job. (Note: To attract the highest pool of candidates, make the job sound attractive. Starbucks can attract a candidate of higher quality in part because it calls its coffee-pourers "baristas.")

- Another paragraph about the company, followed by

- A bulleted list of the essential functions and minimal qualifications for the job.

These are all important, but I suggest adding a fourth paragraph that requires the candidate to tell you something about his or her personality in the cover letter. It might say something like the following:

"In your cover letter, describe your personality. We are looking for someone with the right attitude, who can grow with our company, and who doesn't just want a job ... but wants a job with us. We need to know your personality to know whether you are a fit."

Here is a sample job description:

THE LOCKWOOD COUNTRY CLUB

Tennis Ambassador

About the Position

The Tennis Ambassador position is exclusively dedicated to making the tennis playing experience at Riviera as wonderful as possible for our Members. This means doing whatever it takes to ensure an experience that is second to none – from the cleanliness of the facility to providing the extra service that our members expect and deserve. This position reports to the Director of Tennis Operations.

About The Lockwood Country Club

Opened in 1931, the Lockwood Country Club has a storied history and its championship golf course is world-renowned. The Tennis Club opened in 1967 and has hard, clay, and practice courts, along with programs for all levels of play. We are passionate about the sophisticated elegance of our amenities and service. Our Members enjoy the "Lockwood Lifestyle," which includes the philosophies of Respect Life; Healthy for Life; and Enjoy Life. We're equally passionate about living our vision, mission values, and principles, which start and end with "Only the best is good enough." The vision is embodied in our employees, who are carefully screened, selected, and trained.

About You

You are an outgoing and personable professional with a keen interest in the sports hospitality industry. You understand and live by the concept of being a "team player," making sure that collaboration is essential to your success, as well as the success of those with whom you work. At the same time, you have enough experience and strength to ensure that the right thing is being done. You care innately about people and your goal is to please your members and fellow employees. "It's not in my job description" is not part of your professional vocabulary.

Job Responsibilities

- Meets and greets (by name) members and guests on each court, every hour during the shift.

- Ensures that courts are free of water and debris; that trash is emptied on courts; that water fountains are clean and working. Makes corrections as needed.

- Records guest's name and informs coordinator of guest's presence.

- Offers members and guests available amenities.

- Picks up stray tennis balls around courts and puts them into receptacle bins.

- Picks up stray trash.

- Ensures that restrooms are clean and fully stocked.

- Is responsible for the stocking and cleaning of water stations.

- Checks ball machines frequently to make sure they are working properly.

- Ensures our clay courts are swept and lined.

Knowledge, Skills, and Qualifications

- An abiding love of tennis and sports.

- Ability to interact with clients, co-workers, members, and management in a positive, supportive, and co-operative way.

- Physical ability to walk, see, hear, write, and talk.

- Ability to read, understand, and comply with all safety rules.

The Lockwood Country Club Is an Equal Opportunity Employer.

The most important part of this job description is the section called "About You." This is the part that matters the most to me, and it is the section that requires most of my attention during the interview.

You can post job descriptions on college boards, Monster.com, Craigslist, your own website and social media sites, or through a recruiter.

2. Screening Résumés

The first level of screening can come from the Human Resources Department or Hiring Manager, but afterward, I personally screen all résumés that cross my virtual "desk." Having the right team is just too important to leave it in the hands of someone who is not as personally invested in my company's future. Though I often have an associate to assist me in the process, I always lead the effort.

In this initial screening, I spend about seventy-five or ninety minutes to review every one hundred résumés, and I am generally left with about twenty percent that warrant further scrutiny. Remember, you are looking for two things: 1) minimal requirements; and 2) stand-outs.

Minimal Requirements

I use an applicant tracking system to review résumés. First, I scan them for minimal requirements. This is where ability and experience come into play, and it is usually the last time I consider ability as a component in a hiring decision. For an HR position, the minimal requirements might be: a college degree, ten years of experience, and a certificate in HR.

About four out of every ten résumés will fail to meet the minimal standards.

Stand-Outs

While scanning a résumé, I make note of any features that jump out:

Perhaps the candidate has worked at a company with a particularly strong training program.

- Perhaps the candidate's objective mirrors one of my objectives for my company.

- I love to interview people who attended community college. Perhaps an Ivy-Leaguer will seem more impressive, but I can guarantee this about those individuals who went to community college: They will be hungry and desirous. They *wanted* to go to college. They had a purpose. They have the right attitude, so they can probably learn to be capable.

- In this respect, I'm also looking for people who seem smarter than I. You want a team of people to whom you can turn when you are stuck. So have enough confidence in your own unique abilities that you can surround yourself with extraordinary people.

Remember: A stand-out should jump off the paper and kiss you on the nose!

Warning Signs

Once I have reviewed the remaining résumés, I recruit a team of people to look for warning signs. At this point, we dig a little deeper. Following are some of the warning signs of a bad employee:

- With respect to attitude, I am turned off by social media sites that are hostile, juvenile, or show lack of character.

- A person's attitude might also be reflected in the number of jobs he or she has had. If the employee has had twelve jobs in eight years, you might be dealing with someone whose attitude is difficult. Then again, maybe not. Perhaps the employee is constantly being offered better jobs because her skills are in high demand. Remember, warning signs are just one more tool you are using to evaluate an employee.

- In some cases, being at the same job for twenty years is a warning sign. Is this employee agile? Abreast of the latest developments in his or her field?

- With respect to alignment, look for anything that conflicts with your corporate culture. Let's say someone has a GPA of 4.0 but did not do anything else during his or her entire college experience. This might seem great for your company, but it's a bit of a red flag for me. I want someone who values fun. In fact, at my company, my three big goals are: 1) I want to make a lot of money; 2) I want to have fun; and 3) I want peace and harmony among my own staff. If a candidate doesn't appear to value fun, that candidate is taken out of the running.

- An absence of training or certification indicates that a candidate is not doing anything to further his or her abilities and knowledge. This candidate might not score well in aptitude.

At the end of the day, we have two virtual "piles": candidates who move on to level three, and those we have eliminated from the running. The latter are informed via email.

3. *Phone or Skype Screening*

At this point, all of the candidates who are still in the running are screened via a phone call or video call. I prefer using Skype or Facetime. Nothing replaces an in-person interview for effectiveness, but Skype and Facetime allow you to see features you simply cannot assess via the phone.

I'm not talking about whether the candidates are good-looking, I'm talking about how they present themselves. I have seen it all: infants crying in the background, men wearing wife-beater undershirts, twenty-year-olds who just rolled out of bed.

I am always impressed when people take the calls from their cars while at work. This shows agility. One of my favorite stories dates from when I was teaching two new associates how to interview. We knew the starter-salary position would likely be filled by a recent college graduate, so we had no way to determine ability. When one of our candidates "arrived" for the Skype call, he was clearly in his college dorm room and was wearing a coat and tie.

I abandoned my usual opening question in favor of, "Do you always wear a coat and tie in your dorm room?"

He said, rather shyly, "No, but I thought it was important to make a good impression."

He got called in for another interview, and he eventually landed the job.

The Skype, Facetime, or phone screening usually lasts

five to seven minutes, and it is intended to make sure the candidate fits the minimal standards. For instance:

- The candidate must be eligible to work in the United States.

- The candidate must have a salary requirement that fits within the budget.

The human resources or hiring manager generally conducts this screening for staff members, whereas a partner would conduct the interview for managerial and executive-level positions.

Regardless, I always suggest asking some high-level questions during this phone screening, just so the hiring manager can get a general sense of the person's attitude, aptitude, agility, and alignment. Here are a few of the questions I might ask:

1. "Where would you like to be career-wise in five years?"

2. "Will you give me the five-minute Cliff's Notes version of yourself?"

3. "You've read the job description. Why should you be hired for this position?"

4. "If you won $20 million in the lottery tomorrow, what would you do?"

5. "About thirty-five percent of our new hires don't make it past the ninety-day probationary period. With this figure in mind, if we ask you to come into our office for an interview, will you do it, or

will you be intimidated by this figure?" We ask this question because we want only the best individuals. We want people who are excited to work for us. We don't want to waste our time interviewing people who aren't up for the challenge.

From this screening, a hiring manager is able quickly to gain a lot of insight into the candidate's attitude, agility, aptitude, and alignment. You can tell a lot about a candidate's attitude by listening to the way he or she answers the phone or appears on Skype/Facetime. The hiring manager can also tell a little bit about his or her level of agility. How quickly does the person "snap into gear" when he or she realizes that a potential employer is calling on the other line?

Generally speaking, the pool of candidates is reduced by about fifty percent from this phone screening alone. Candidates who do not make it past this level are notified via email. The remaining candidates are sent an employment application via email and are invited to a first-level interview.

4. First-Level Interview

A first-level interview is tough. You should expect it to be. As I've said throughout this book, take your time and take care when interviewing. Plan on having the candidate spend three or four hours with your team. Ask questions I have included in this book, as well as your own follow-up questions that are relevant to the position and the candidate. Remember: There is no Bible for interview questions. You must be the investigator who determines which questions to ask based on your company and the position available.

I like to have a variety of current managers or employees conduct first-level interviews. This might be a hiring manager (the person to whom the employee will directly report), a peer of that manager, and two to three employees who would be peers of the new employees.

My reasoning is this:

1. I want as many eyes as possible on a potential employee. I think I am a fantastic evaluator of talent, but I'm not perfect: I'm going to "whiff" about fifteen to twenty percent of the time.

2. I like using interviews as a way of developing my existing high-potential employees. I want those same individuals to be interviewing and meeting candidates; they are closer to the job than we are, they can provide more accurate information, and they are more likely to understand what is needed in an employee than I do. Plus, sitting in on interviews starts developing them as future leaders.

Generally speaking, this first round of interviews results in a four- or five-person pool of candidates. Candidates who do not make it past this level are notified by phone call or personalized email. The remaining candidates are sent instructions to complete a screening test.

One of the most frequently asked questions I get is some variation of, "What is the best screening test for candidates?"

It's a good question, but unfortunately there is no correct answer. I've seen every permutation of screen known to man over the past thirty years, from Myers-Briggs, to Kolbe, to the new generation of automated fit to culture. Most of them are helpful, but none of them is perfect.

In fact, people tend to rely too much on these programs. They are tools to help you make informed decisions, but they are not the decision-makers themselves. Decisions must come from you. In fact, I see many of these systems validate bad behavior. I can't tell you the number of times a quality person has been told by a program to never go into sales, only to have what would have been a tremendous salesperson turn his back on a career, as if an oracle came by and deemed it so.

After all of that, we arrive at the second interview.

5. Second-Level Interview

This is usually the final interview. All candidates will be interviewed by the same people. Note that I wrote "people."

This interview—or rather, set of interviews—generally takes about four hours. I suggest doing an in-depth second-level interview for every single person you hire, from the part-time assistant to the senior-level executives. Obviously, the group of people involved in interviewing a candidate who is applying for an executive position will be different from the group of people involved in interviewing a candidate applying as a part-time assistant, but finding the right fit is equally important in each case. I have seen more than one part-time employee sink a ship. In fact, it's generally not the senior-level executives who are betraying a company and stirring up trouble. Their jobs are harder to come by. Part-time assistants can likely pick up a comparable job with much more ease, so they are much more likely to be cavalier about their employment.

I suggest including multiple people in this process because I know from experience that different people see different things. You are more likely to get a bigger picture of a candidate if you have multiple people offering varied perspectives.

Yes, it's more work to involve multiple people in a four-hour interview process, and it can cause some hassles when you have a bunch of cooks in one kitchen. If you do the work up front, though, you will save loads of hassles when it comes time to manage your new employee.

The second-level interview looks something like this:

- The candidate arrives at about 10:30 a.m. and is given an itinerary for the day.

- He or she is taken to a conference room and offered coffee.

- The first interview occurs at about 10:40 a.m. and lasts thirty minutes. During this interview, a key manager asks questions that specifically elicit information about the candidate's agility, attitude, aptitude, and alignment.

- The candidate has a five- or ten-minute break before the second interview.

- The second interview occurs at about 11:15 a.m. and lasts another thirty minutes. Again, a key manager asks questions intended to bring to light information about the candidate's agility, attitude, aptitude, and alignment.

- At about 11:45 a.m., the candidate is given a tour of the office by the director of human resources.

During this tour, the director of human resources is assessing the candidate.

- At noon, two employees take the candidate to lunch.

- Finally, the candidate returns to another thirty-minute interview by a key manager.

During each step, the candidate is being assessed in the Five A's, with specific attention being placed on agility, attitude, aptitude, and alignment. By this point, we usually know quite a bit about the candidate's ability, so our focus is on the intangibles.

Key managers are generally given a few stock interview questions to get the ball rolling, but ninety percent of the conversation is free-flowing. They want to "go deep" and ask questions based on the candidate's response. Such an interview requires a lot of role-playing and preparation in advance.

When hiring for the Five A's, use the questions that you have seen throughout this book, and come up additional questions of your own that are specific to your company and the candidate. Use off-the-wall questions to determine agility; ask broad, open-ended questions to determine attitude and ability. Ask them what they know about your business and your culture to determine aptitude and alignment.

The human resources director and lunch buddies (peers) are usually looking closely at alignment. When the human resources director gives the candidate a tour, the candidate probably relaxes a little bit, showing his or her true self. The human resources director is assessing how easily he or she can establish rapport. What is the dynamic? Does the candidate easily connect with the employees he or she is meeting?

You likely already have very friendly employees who can establish rapport with just about anyone. The human resources director should pay close attention to how well the candidate is able to communicate with these employees. It's natural for a candidate to be a little shy and reserved during this process, but if he or she is unable to make small talk even with the Chatty Cathys and Affable Andys in your office, he or she will probably have a very difficult time establishing rapport with some of the more difficult personality types that might flood into your office in the form of vendors, customers, or even peers. He or she might lack agility.

The same goes for the lunch with peers. Hopefully, the candidate will speak more freely with peers than with people seen as superiors. Likewise, my employees will ask questions that I would never think to ask. We always send extremely loyal employees who understand that: 1) They are on the clock doing important reconnaissance work for the team; and 2) We value and need their input.

6. Assessing and Hiring a Candidate

The key managers, human resources director, and peers responsible for assessing the candidate all fill out simple forms, as shown later in this chapter. Once the candidate leaves, the team members are reminded not to discuss the candidate until every single candidate has been interviewed.

It's easy to fall in love with the first person you interview, and it's also easy to give another team member information that influences his or her opinion of a candidate. When we finally meet to discuss all the candidates, we want everyone's opinion to be as pure and personal as possible, so we have a rule against discussing candidates until we are sitting at the table ready to make a decision.

When the hiring team — which includes all the people who interviewed, toured, had lunch with, or otherwise assessed the candidate — meets to make the decision, the first thing we do is ask six questions. For each question, we go around the room and have everyone participating in the process answer these questions, rating the candidates on a scale of one to three:

1. "How likely would you be to hire this candidate?"

2. "How much ability do you think this candidate has?"

3. "How agile is this candidate?"

4. "How is this candidate's attitude?"

5. "How much aptitude does this candidate display?"

6. "How well aligned is this candidate?"

We also ask all the participants to explain their rating. I went through this process about six months ago with a client's hiring team. The first five people answered the first question with raving reviews. They would all hire this candidate. Then came Stephen's answer: "I give this candidate a one. I would not hire him. He arrived in a suit coat that was dirty. If he cannot go the trouble to clean his suit coat before an interview, what do you think his attitude will be toward providing high-quality work?"

Stephen had a point—and it was something the rest of us had never seen.

Once everyone has assessed the candidate and had the opportunity to listen to everyone else's feedback, we tally each candidate's score, announce the scores, and then ask everyone to choose one person he or she would hire if the decision were his or hers alone.

In a perfect world, we will have consensus. When we are divided, we have a Skype call with all of the candidates in question so that we can dig up more information.

When a final candidate is selected, he is contacted via telephone, and then sent a conditional job offer by email. The job offer is contingent upon a background check, including calls to prior employers and a reference check.

Once the candidate passes a background check, the offer is confirmed, and the other candidates are notified via a signed letter from their main point of contact.

The employee is now ready to be managed by a rockstar manager trained in the Five A's.

Rating for Candidate John Q. Smith

	Manager / Partner	Manager / Partner	Human Resources Director	Peer	Peer	Manager / Partner
Ability: Will he/she be able to perform all aspects of the position?						
Agility: Can he/she make the necessary adjustment to be successful?						
Attitude: Would you enjoy working with this person?						
Aptitude: Does he/she have the competency to be successful?						
Alignment: Will he/she fit in? Would you want to get a drink with this person?						
Overall						

APPENDIX B

PERFORMANCE AND CULTIVATION PREVIEWS

At heart, performance and cultivation previews should be a conversation between a boss and an employee to improve performance. They are not technical or administrative. It is a two-way conversation, and it must be driven from the top down. If performance and cultivation previews cannot be used effectively and be baked into the DNA of your corporate culture, stop doing them. They are a waste of time.

When done properly, they are a subjective and effective way to make an employee about twenty percent more productive.

Did I just write the word *subjective*? Yes, yes, I did. Performance reviews started back in the 1950s as a way to deal with union requirements. They were an objective way to measure employees across the board.

We no longer have assembly lines of employees all doing the same tedious task. We have companies built on relationships, where customers can ruin a company in a day or two by posting bad reviews on Yelp and social media sites.

The world has changed, and so too must the performance review — hence the term performance *preview*.

Under the performance and cultivation previews, you realize that your employees are unique individuals with different skills and different responsibilities, and so your conversation with each of them is also different. The performance and cultivation previews are interactive, which makes them subjective by definition. And remember: Your top performers *should be treated differently from your worst performers*. When you decide to treat top performers and bottom performers in the same way, one of two things can happen: 1) You treat the top performers worse than they should be treated; and/or 2) You treat the bottom performers better than they should be treated. The only person who can possibly win in this scenario is your worst employee.

So expect your performance and cultivation previews to be subjective. Expect that you will give more to your top performers. It might not seem fair to your employees, but it is most certainly just and it serves your company well.

I suggest the following protocol for conducting performance reviews:

1. Start your performance and cultivation previews by talking to your best employees. Most employers want to get the ugly ones out of the way, but when you start with your worst employees, they go around spreading poison and toxicity all over the place. When you kick off your performance and cultivation previews by talking to the best employees, they come out feeling happy and

energetic. It creates a corporate culture where performance and cultivation previews are fun, something to look forward to.

The performance and cultivation previews consists of: 1) a stay interview; 2) an employee self-review; 3) a review; and 4) a next-steps discussion. We will go through these one at a time.

2. After an employee has a performance and cultivation preview, give him or her four hours the following day to reflect on what she or she has done and what he or she will do in the following year or quarter. Harvard found that if you give employees this four-hour time to reflect on the performance and cultivation previews, they will come back about twenty percent more productive!*

The Stay Interview

Think of a stay interview a little like reviewing your wedding vows. The employee confirms that he or she wants to continue working at the organization, and the employee-employer bond is strengthened so that both parties understand and commit to certain goals.

The stay interview starts with a questionnaire that the employee completes prior to the performance and cultivation preview. The manager will review the document in preparation for the actual interview, which takes place during the review.

---

*   Nobel, C. (2014, May 5). Reflecting on Work Improves Job Performance. *Harvard Business School*. Retrieved from http:// hbswk.hbs.edu/item/7509.html

When stay interviews are incorporate into the performance and cultivation preview environment, employees and employers can find commonalities and reflect on shared goals.

Employee Self-Review

Knowing how an employee rates his or her own performance is as important as knowing how you rate his or her performance. For one thing, it gives the employee a voice. It also asks an employee to be honest and introspective. Imagine this difference: The employee is called into a room for his performance preview. During the meeting, the manager tells the employee that he is not performing as expected when it comes to communicating with team members. The employee feels defensive. At best, he leaves the meeting feeling lousy. At worst, he argues, creating a downward spiral that spreads toxicity.

Now imagine that he is given a chance to provide his own self-review. Because he knows he is going to sit in front of a manager and compare notes, he truly considers all aspects of his job. He realizes that he is not a great team member sometimes.

During the performance preview, his manager says, "I noticed that one of the areas we both think you can improve is in communicating with your team. Let's brainstorm now about some of the ways you can do this."

Now the focus is on the solution. Both the employee and the employer feel empowered. The employee does not feel attacked. Rather, he feels like he and his manager are on the same team.

Self-evaluations are important because they help management see things through their employees' eyes. If a manager and an employee have a giant disparity in how they see a person's performance, great! The manager can say something like, "It's not always easy for me to understand what is happening in the trenches. I notice that you gave yourself a five out of five in this area, and I gave you a three. Obviously, I'm not seeing what is happening from your perspective. Tell me more."

The employer might learn something about the company and how it works. Perhaps an employee seems inefficient, but he's actually spending a ton of time dealing with workflow issues that have to do more with a company's systems than with his or her efficiency.

Or, perhaps not. Maybe the employee is trying to pass the buck. This tells you something about the employee's character, which is also important to know! When you work to determine ways to change the differences in perception, you are telling the employee: *You are expected to perform, no matter what.* You can also say something akin to this directly to the employee, "Thank you for sharing your perception. Here is a solution that I suggest. We need you to be more efficient, so if this solution does not work, or if you disagree that this solution will work, please come to me immediately."

Review

Next up is the actual review. This is where you sit with the employee and discuss what has happened and what you expect to happen next year.

Again, it is helpful to think of this as a cultivation preview. I'm calling it a review to differentiate this step in the overall performance and cultivation preview process, but it is helpful to think of this as a cultivation preview.

The review starts by your discussing the stay-interview questionnaire. If the employee wants to stay with your company, this should be fun. Your employee gets to talk about his or her future goals.

Next up is a discussion of the self-evaluation as it compares to the employer's observations.

And finally, and most importantly, is your discussion of the Five A's as they pertain to the employee's performance. It is impossible to train attitude, aptitude, and agility, but ability and alignment can be coached. And a person who is fundamentally a happy person, but who suddenly has a bad attitude, should be given an opportunity to try to resolve the conflict.

This is what the review looks like:

1. Explain the Five A's to your employee. It helps to also hand him or her a piece of paper that explains the Five A's. This is included in the Appendix.

2. Explain how you have rated your employee in each of the areas, and why. A deeper explanation of this conversation can be found in this appendix after the Sample Performance and Cultivation Preview form.

3. Give the employee a physical summary of his or her review. Following is a blank review form.

Sample Performance and Cultivation Preview

ABC Company Employee Performance and Cultivation Review		
Employee Name:	Date:	Reviewer:

Ability: Describe the employee's productivity, accuracy, reliability, and professionalism.

Agility: Describe the employee's readiness to change, effectiveness when required to change, and independence and personal leadership skills.

Alignment: How well is the employee aligned with the mission, vision, values, culture, and goals of ABC Company?

Attitude: How is the employee's attitude? How well does the employee communicate? Is the employee a team player? Proactive and supportive? Does the employee possess heroic competence?

Aptitude: Describe the employee's willingness and ability to learn, as well as his or her skills, experience development, exercise of grit, insight, and awareness.

Rating Scale

5 = Significantly Above Standard. Exceptional performance at all times.

4 = Above Standard. Exceeds expectations in most areas.

3 = Standard. Meets expectations in all areas.

2 = Below Standard. Does not meet standards in all areas.

1 = Significantly Below Standard. Performance consistently does not meet expectations.

Standard	Rating
Ability	
Agility	
Alignment	

Attitude	
Aptitude	
OVERALL PERFORMANCE RATING	

Agreed-Upon Next Steps:

1.

2.

3.

4.

5.

Employee Signature:	**Date:**

This review is the same for any employee—from assistant to manager, but we add one category for managers only: turnover. A company's success is contingent on its managers' ability to hire well. One of my clients hired me because it needed to staff nine hundred employees at any one time, but of the past three hundred employees who were hired, half either quit or were fired. One of the changes I made when I came on board was that I began holding the hiring managers accountable for turnover.

Explaining Your Employee's Rating

Ninety percent of the performance preview should be focused on the next year. The problem with most performance reviews is that they focus on the previous year, on what has already happened. It is hard for your employees to feel motivated by reviewing all their past mistakes, so in almost every case, the conversation should be about how the employee can raise his or her game.

Employees are given a one to five in each of the Five A's. An employee who receives a three is an employee who is meeting standards. An employee who receives a five is an employee who knocks your socks off and delights you at every single opportunity. An employee who receives a one in any given area should be fired immediately.

Most employees will, therefore, receive threes. These employees are not going to be fired, but they also are not going to be on the fast track to promotion. During the review, a manager should define what a four needs to look like. (A four is someone who is exceeding expectations almost every day in every way.) Do not sugarcoat anything. Focus on what the employee needs to do to raise himself or herself to the next level. Giving your employee clear directions is the only way to set the employee up for success.

Here are some explanations you can give your employees about the rating system. Appendix C includes a one-sheet explanation which you can copy and give to your employees prior to their performance and cultivation reviews.

What Is a Five?

A five indicates exceptional performance at all times. There is no room for improvement; when you assign a five, your employee cannot do his or her job any better in that category.

For instance, an employee who scores a five comes into work with a great attitude every single day, constantly thinking about ways he or she can help improve the company. This means that you don't know the day or time that she does not possess and live with a positive attitude. Even when things are really, really tough, that person maintains an exceptional attitude.

That person may not be a five in every category, but in that one category, this person is exceptional. What's more, everybody in the company knows that that individual is a five in attitude. When you begin talking about that person's attitude at a recognition event or in a team meeting, all the employees start nodding their heads in understanding of the fact that in that one category, the employee is exceptional, almost perfect.

Therefore, assigning a five should happen rarely.

What Is a Four?

A four is above standard, meaning that person exceeds expectations most of the time. A person who receives a four in a category is very good in most areas within that category, but he is not perfect.

For example, if a person has a very good attitude most of the time, but shows up with low energy when his six-week-old baby has kept him up until the wee hours of the morning, that person is given a four.

Does that seem harsh? You might be thinking, *The poor guy has a new baby at home. Cut him some slack.*

You would never fire an employee for receiving a four. That employee would be celebrated. The fours are reserved for the upper twenty percent of your team.

And while it might seem harsh to judge a person based on a six-week-old baby's behavior, remember that we are talking about performance. Performance can and does change based on circumstances. Your employees want you to be honest and set expectations. You are not expecting your employee to show up with high energy when his baby keeps him up at night. Remember: a four exceeds expectations.

What Is a Three?

The most important thing to remember about a three is that it is not a bad number. Most employees will receive threes in most areas. It reflects a job well done. Managers need to know how to communicate this.

The explanation of a three might look like this:

"We are defining a three, throughout our organization, as a good employee. This is like winning a bronze medal in the Olympics. It is pretty darn awesome. It means you are doing a good job each and every day. You were not rated exceptional, because that is reserved for the very top employees. Let me give you some examples of why I rated you a three. However, there is nothing for you to be upset about. We think you are doing an overall good job. We are happy to have you here. "

Once you give a few examples of how the employee met performance, you can spend most of the conversation focusing on what that person can do to become a four or a five, if he or she wants to work that hard.

If a person barely squeaked out a three and you need for the employee to raise his or her game, the conversation should be focused as follows: "I debated long and hard as to whether to give you a two or not. Next year, if nothing improves, it will be a two."

What Is a Two?

A two is someone who needs improvement, and needs improvement right away. It should not come as a surprise to the employee that he or she is receiving a two in any given category. This is a person who has performance issues that have been discussed at length and more than once prior to the performance and cultivation previews.

This means the employee is simply not doing his or her job in an adequate way. There is nothing special about this employee. He or she shows up and goes through the motions but does not usually meet your expectations.

It is important to note that there are two types of twos: those who are ascending, and those who are descending. It is important to delineate between them. Someone who is working hard to improve should receive credit in the review process for taking these steps. The conversation should be focused on ways to continue to improve. It might sound like this:

"You are getting better. I cannot honestly tell you that you are where you need to be because you are not.

However, I do see improvement and it encourages me. What do you think you need to do to become a three?"

Give the employee some examples. Focus on the people who are threes, fours, and fives. Make a determination whether this employee truly wants to improve and be the employee you need him to be, or if this will be a continued struggle over the next year or two. No one has enough time to struggle with an employee for a year or two. Tell that to the employee.

If the person is descending, the conversation is different. This person should probably resign or be terminated. Here is how the conversation might sound:

"Despite the fact that we've had conversations about your performance in this area, your performance is unacceptable. Here are the examples of what I am talking about. I want you to honestly look in the mirror in the next few days and decide if you can change enough to warrant continued employment here. If you cannot, we need to move on. Let's have a conversation about this after the weekend."

What Is a One?

Candidly, a one is somebody who should already have been fired. Any one in any category is unacceptable in my organization. If one of my managers gave an employee a one during the review process, I would seriously question why the manager had not yet terminated the employee.

If at any time, an employee does something that falls into the category of one performance, the employee should be given immediate feedback from the manager with disciplinary action associated. If this happens once during a year, I allow one more chance, but if this person cannot improve within thirty days, he or she will need to find employment elsewhere.

Next Steps

Thirty days following the performance and cultivation preview, call your employees back for a Next Steps meeting. At this point, you can discuss improvement and status with your employees.

This Next Steps gives teeth to your performance and cultivation previews. It tells your employees that the performance and cultivation previews mean something and are to be taken seriously.

APPENDIX C

EXPLANING THE FIVE A's TO YOUR EMPLOYEES

Ability

In this category, we are looking primarily for your ability to do your job well. What is your level of productivity? How accurate is your work? Are you reliable— meaning, can we count on you to arrive on time and to complete tasks within deadlines? What is your level of professionalism?

Agility

In order to get to the next level, great employees need to be agile; this means you can adapt, evolve, and get downright GRITTY. Examples would be to take on new assignments, stop in the middle of one task to help someone else with another task, or bring together several people to make something work. Agility is the power of moving as quickly as needed. Are you able to support management needs to act rapidly when the need arises? Do you do it with a "bring-it-on" look on your face? When you are taking on a more complex or new project, are you able to dig in and try to learn as much as possible before asking for help? When change is announced, are you able to quickly and courageously adapt to that change, or are you one of those people who are reluctant to change?

Alignment

We need our employees to be aligned with our mission, vision, culture, values, and goals. What is the reaction of the people you work with every day to you? If you're in customer service, do your customers thank you at the end of an interaction? Are vendors or dealers appreciative of what you do? Are you an evangelist four our company? Since our mission is to improve lives (of our people and the people we serve and partner with), how do you do that? Are you able to articulate and demonstrate what our mission, vision, values, culture, and goals are? Do you connect with people who are physically challenged and want to improve their lives?

Attitude

Your attitude is exceptionally important, because it's really something we cannot coach, manage, or change, yet it has a profound ripple effect throughout the entire company. A great attitude goes a long way in determining if you will have a long career path here. We look for employees who are courageous, fearless, and relentlessly positive; we want employees who seek solutions rather than complain about problems. We value team players who are always willing to help out a colleague in any way possible, whether it's offering to help carry a box to the car or serving as a sounding board for a customer service problem. Not everyone can have a great attitude every day, but the employee who is significantly above expectations has that positive attitude a vast majority of the time, and is able to mask those few days when things aren't so great. What would fellow employees, customers, and partners say about your attitude? Ultimately your attitude is solely determined by you. It's your choice, every day.

Aptitude

"Aptitude" means the ability or capacity for achieving something, measured generally by how effectively a person can learn. We want aptitude to be taken to a higher level. Are you aware of what's happening at our company and in our industry? Are you an expert? Do you understand your role as part of a bigger, strategic picture? Closely tied to attitude, this category also means the ability to take calculated risks and get in the trenches to gain the knowledge and aptitude that can be gained only through experience—sometimes challenging, uncertain, and uncomfortable experiences. When there is a problem, a person with great aptitude finds a way to solve it and even discovers a new opportunity. It's a lot easier to simply say *no*. Whether addressing a customer service complaint or a logistical challenge in the warehouse, great employees find a way to say *yes* or *let's see what we can do.*

About the Author

Eric Swenson's career in management and leadership has spanned more than twenty-five years, during which time he has interviewed more than five thousand candidates for jobs and has analyzed every permutation of questions, skills tests, personality evaluations, and formula ever invented.

When working for large corporations, he knew innately that the hiring process was important. But it was only when he started his own business that he realized how critical a great hire was. When he was interviewing his first employee, he knew he could not afford to make a mistake. As a result, he spent far more time researching, interviewing, asking for references, and asking respected colleagues to spend time with the candidates than did any of his past employers. He could not afford to make a mistake, so he made sure that he did not.

Hiring a great employee was a transformational experience. Eric began studying what makes a great employee, and just how critical it is never to make a mistake in hiring.

Eric started his own consulting firm in 2003, and has worked with hundreds of businesses throughout North

America, providing Human Resources, talent management, and leadership development outsourcing and training. He's a sought-after speaker on topics such as the above.

Eric lives in Los Angeles.

www.ericwswenson.com